Your Assignment is Greater Than Your Affliction

Darrin Monroe

EDITED BY

Nicole Queen

VISION PUBLISHING
HOUSE

Vision Publishing House
support@vision-publishinghouse.com
www.vision-publishinghouse.com

ISBN: 979-8-9933667-5-3 (print)
LCCN: 2025923742

This book is established to provide information and inspiration to all readers. It is designed with the understanding that the author is not engaged to render any psychological, legal, or any other kind of professional advice. The content is the sole expression of the author. The author is not liable for any physical, psychological, emotional, financial, or commercial damages, including, but not limited to special, incidental, consequential, or other damages. All readers are responsible for their own choices, actions, and results.

To my wife, Lawren—the steady rhythm in every measure of my life—and to our children, Aaron, Rose, Stephanie, and Trinity, the joyful melody that keeps it all in tune. Love you all to LIFE!

"For our light affliction, which is but for a moment, worketh for us a far more exceeding and eternal weight of glory."

— 2 Corinthians 4:17 (KJV)

CONTENTS

FOREWORD

Grace, mercy, and peace beyond to you from God,
our father and the Lord Jesus Christ.

There are moments in life when heaven leans in and breathes on a
message that was not born from comfort, but forged in the furnace of
affliction. This book, *Your Assignment Is Greater Than Your Affliction*, is
one of those divine moments. It carries the fragrance of suffering, the
oil of perseverance, and the revelation of a man who has chosen
calling over comfort, faith over feeling, and assignment over
affliction.

I have watched my son Darrin in the Spirit. He has walked a real
journey not the kind that looks polished on the outside, but the kind
that presses, stretches, and refines a person into a vessel God can
trust. Darren has learned not merely to survive affliction, but to inter-
pret it through the lens of divine purpose.

His testimony echoes the words of the apostle Paul:

 For our light affliction, which is but for a moment, is

working for us a far more exceeding and eternal weight
of glory.

— 2 CORINTHIANS 4:17

Affliction does not cancel assignment it clarifies it. It does not weaken
faith, it works faith. It does not bury destiny, it builds it. Every chapter
in this book will remind you that pain is not punishment; it is preparation. That trials are not setbacks; they are training grounds for
glory.

Darrin writes not as a theorist, but as a witness. He has seen the
God who steadies trembling hands, the God who lifts the weary heart,
the God who whispers purpose in the midst of pressure, and the God
who proves Himself faithful when life feels unfair. In these pages, you
will discover that the same grace that carries him is available to
carry you.

As you read, expect your faith to rise. Expect clarity to return.
Expect strength to re-enter your spirit. Expect to be reminded that
your story is not over, your oil is not empty, and your assignment is
still alive even if your soul has walked through fire.

No affliction can stop what God has ordained. No season of pain
can erase your identity. Destiny does not bow to difficulty; difficulty
bows to destiny.

I bless this work. I bless this assignment. And I bless every reader
who dares to believe again, to stand again, to fight again, and to finish
what God started in them.

Your assignment remains greater. Your calling remains sure. Your
future remains bright. And your God remains faithful.

With love and kingdom pride,

Bishop George C. Searight
Abundant Life Family Worship Church

PREFACE

As a young church musician growing up, I remember sitting at that old upright piano wondering, "What hymn would they be opening with on this beautiful, sunny Sunday morning?" Then, it happened: someone would just start singing, "Time is filled with swift transitions..."

As you would expect, at 14 years old, I had no idea what that line in the song meant. Well, now I truly understand. The year 2020 will always be a year in my mind that was transitional on so many different levels.

As a pastor of a thriving church, I remember being excited about this year. I had been in prayer about the direction of the ministry and what would be the next assignment that God would give us to do. I'm always excited to hear a Word from the Lord as it relates to serving His children and building His Kingdom.

My ears were so attentive. Would we do more outreach? Enhance our deaf ministry? Build up our youth and young adults? The things I was seeing and feeling in my heart were endless. I personally felt that zeal that I had when I first started pastoring. I couldn't wait to share the things I was hearing with my congregation.

With growing expectations, I felt as though we were about to embark on something that we had never seen or done before. It would be innovative, refreshing, and life-changing. I was also inspired by the themes that I heard so many pastors sharing. They were proclaiming that 2020 would be the year of *perfect vision*, or the *year of new vision*, and so many others.

However, when I began to seek God for the direction for the church I pastored, I just kept hearing in my spirit: *The Year of REFO-CUS*. I pondered this thought for weeks. Why refocus? Refocus on what?

Well, I followed what the Lord was saying to me and then I announced it to the congregation: "2020 will be the year of REFO-CUS." At that moment, it all started coming to me. It was time for God's people to refocus their attention back to the things that please God — refocus on God, Jesus, the Holy Spirit, relationships, righteous living, prayer, worship, praise, forgiveness, and everything that is right in God's eyes.

Yes, we had become so distracted with life that we had begun to drift away from the One who gave us life. It was now time to return to our first love, and that is our heavenly Father and His Son Jesus.

How to Use This Book

This book was designed to be an experience you live. Each chapter was prayerfully written to help you recognize that your *assignment* is not limited by your *affliction*, but refined through it.

As you move through each page, you'll find yourself invited into a rhythm of *Reflection, Action,* and *Declaration,* which is a process that transforms understanding into movement, and movement into growth.

Reflection

Each chapter concludes with questions that are meant to help you pause and look inward. *Reflection* allows you to quiet the noise around you and truly hear what God is saying about your situation. Don't rush this part. Find a quiet space, pray, and journal your responses honestly. The goal isn't perfection; it's awareness. As you reflect, you'll begin to see patterns, lessons, and divine fingerprints on every part of your journey.

Action

After reflection comes response. The *Action* section invites you to move from revelation to application. Here, you'll be challenged to take practical steps: writing, planning, organizing, or initiating change. Think of these as your spiritual assignments for each chapter. Every action you take reinforces your faith and strengthens your ability to stay focused, disciplined, and determined throughout the process.

Declaration

Finally, each chapter closes with a *Declaration*. This a spoken word of faith that aligns your mouth with your mission. Declarations are affirmations; they are prophetic confessions that reshape how you think, believe, and walk. Speak them out loud with boldness. Declare them until they become part of your *language of victory*.

How to Journey Through

You can read this book chapter by chapter in order, or you can begin wherever you feel led. However, for the greatest impact, give each section time to settle in your spirit before moving on. Some readers may spend a day or even a week on a single chapter. They may focus on rereading, journaling, and revisiting the *Reflection*, *Action*, and *Declaration* sections as they evolve.

Please remember that this is *not* a race; it's a refining process. Every page is an opportunity for God to reveal, realign, and reignite your focus.

So grab your journal, open your heart, and commit to walking through this journey with expectation. As you do, you'll discover that every challenge was preparation, and that...

Your assignment is greater than your affliction!

INTRODUCTION

I am always asked the question:

How are you able to maintain a balance as a full-time pastor, a committed family man, and a career-driven corporate executive?

So many individuals have said to me over the years that it seems very challenging to effectively manage each of these responsibilities without losing focus on who you are as a person and becoming overwhelmed. I fully agree and understand their point of view. Yes, the demands can be great and sometimes extremely difficult and daunting; however, it is the rewards that are so fulfilling to me, along with the valuable life lessons learned, that will always help me to overcome in any future tests or trials.

For me, the key is understanding what your assignments in life are —being confident in your purpose and reason for being created. It's key to understand that you are not an accident or an afterthought. Everyone on earth has a purpose, but not everyone will take the time to focus on it and put the necessary elements in place to accomplish it.

I fully recognize that, in life, there are so many distractions coming at us, but at the same time, there are greater opportunities awaiting us. Being confident in your ability to continually reach the desired goals and achievements is paramount—fighting hard to maintain enough self-discipline in order to avoid being overtaken by any circumstances that may enter into our lives.

It's imperative that you always stay in a posture of faith:

 "For we walk by faith, not by sight."

— 2 CORINTHIANS 5:7

This means that we're always moving forward because of what we believe to be successfully achievable, and not by the negative environment around us that, many times, will be magnified by our five senses.

I've learned to distance myself from distractions and now focus on the expected outcome. Being clear on your assignment and calling in life is so vital, not only to ourselves but also to the people and environments around us. There is always a consequence to every action or word we project.

So the question is: *how do we continue to move forward with urgency to complete that assignment when it seems as though there are so many obstacles in our way?*

It is my prayer that God will use this book to help propel you into full confidence that you are able to successfully navigate through your God-given assignments in life. Too many times we quit, give up, and throw in the towel because we feel that the weight of it all is difficult to bear. With this I say: anything worth having is worth fighting for.

In this book, I share with you some principles that God has shared with me. These principles will teach you how to keep progressing toward the desired goal of completion, even when it's a struggle to do so. There is a fight in you that you haven't even tapped into yet. It's this fight that will get you to the next level—the place where you will look back and give God all the glory and praise for helping you execute a win once again.

God has equipped you with everything you need to get the job done. I just need you to know: *You Won.* Did you notice the language of faith I just released? *"You Won!"* Don't lose heart and take the easy way out by taking shortcuts. The victory is in the press and the lessons that you have learned through each experience.

There is glory on the other side of this. This is your season! This is your moment! Your assignment is greater than your affliction.

* * *

Now that you've read this chapter, take time to sit with what God has revealed. This is your time to connect what you've read to where you are, and where God is leading you next. Use the following page to reflect, write, and respond.

REFLECTION

1. Where do I sense a God-given assignment stirring right now?

_____
_____
_____
_____

2. What distractions most often pull me off-purpose?

_____
_____
_____
_____

3. How has God used past afflictions to teach me?

_____
_____
_____
_____

ACTION

Identify your core purpose for this season and begin aligning your daily choices with it. Recognize three distractions that often pull you off course and set clear boundaries to keep your focus strong.

DECLARATION

Say this declaration with conviction. Let it remind you who you are and what God has called you to do.

I am created on purpose for purpose.
I begin this journey with focus and faith.

Chapter 1

Affliction

"Many are the afflictions of the righteous, but the Lord delivereth him out of them all."

— Psalm 34:19

So often when I heard the word *affliction*, I would immediately think of something associated with a sickness or debilitating disease. It was something that came to cause physical harm to our bodies both internally and externally. However, as I began to look at afflictions from a much deeper viewpoint, I found that afflictions extended far beyond my current understanding. I agree that an affliction is something that causes pain and suffering; however, it can affect us physically, emotionally, and yes, even spiritually.

At some point in our lives, each one of us will be introduced to some level of affliction. Affliction can manifest itself in many forms. As I've already stated, it can be a sickness or disease, but it can also come as feelings of loneliness, stress, fear, grief, depression, and even anxiety. It can become an inability to move forward in life, a feeling of being trapped in a particular socioeconomic status, and even spiritual stagnancy. Spiritual stagnancy is a place where you may feel as though you've hit a brick wall in your walk with Christ.

Let's take this even deeper. There are times when the pressure to perform and meet the approval and opinions of others will cause us self-afflictions. Self-affliction occurs when we are so hard on ourselves to be accepted and liked by everyone, and when that doesn't happen, we immediately think that there is something wrong with us. Listen, afflictions have one major objective, and that is to paralyze us in our tracks so that the purpose and destiny God has designed for our lives are not given the chance to mature to their fullest potential.

In order for you and me to be in a position to overcome afflictions, I want you to first recognize and understand that afflictions always seem to show up when we're at the threshold of something great. This is the reason we should be encouraged and excited whenever we are faced with an affliction. It is a clear and precise indicator that you are getting closer to fulfilling another seasonal assignment that God has planned for your life. As a matter of fact, let's say it this way: when we are experiencing afflictions of any nature, let's change our perception and perspective of what we are experiencing. We will not view what we are going through as a problem but instead as an opportunity that will lead to some of the greatest God-moves in our lives.

Every affliction we encounter will validate and reveal the unlimited potential that many times has been waiting to be awakened. It creates a place for us to actively participate in our spiritual growth and maturity. These are the moments in our lives that are designed to produce the seeds of greatness and success that have been planted within us. We were designed to win, and whatever it takes to get us to the winner's circle, we will arrive!

The Word of God says:

> For your sake we are killed every day;
> we are being slaughtered like sheep.
> No, despite all these things,
> overwhelming victory is ours through Christ,

who loved us.

— Romans 8:36–37 (NLT)

The trials and tribulations we have to go through are all a part of the process. However, we must remain encouraged because we know that we will always have overwhelming victory. The victory on the other side of the affliction is decisive and absolute. According to the Word of God, we are guaranteed the win. The Bible states:

 "No weapon formed against you will prosper."

— Isaiah 54:17 (KJV)

The experiences that you gain while going through afflictions are essential to your growth and maturity. This is the place where God is developing us. Development is defined as the process that creates growth and positive change. Something positive is going to come out of those seasons where we are faced with afflictions.

Let's take a look at Romans:

 We can rejoice, too, when we run into problems and trials, for we know that they help us develop endurance. And endurance develops strength of character, and character strengthens our confident hope of salvation. And this hope will not lead to disappointment. For we know how dearly God loves us, because he has given us the Holy Spirit to fill our hearts with his love.

— Romans 5:3–5 (NLT)

In life, not only will we experience rocket-ship moments where we are steadily climbing to higher altitudes, but there will be times that will feel like we're on a roller coaster. It will be filled with many ups and downs, twists and turns. It's here where you will be introduced to feelings of frustration, pain, and discouragement. Even though this is a tough place to be in, many times our private pain is God's way of preparing us for a public promotion. You are becoming stronger due to the resistance that you are feeling.

The exciting thing to note is that God is going to receive all the glory through what you are going through. Now you have a powerful testimony that can be shared with someone else to help them through their moments of afflictions and struggles. This is how you know that the afflictions are maturing us. There is a lesson to be learned. Look at it this way: in this painful season you are dealing with, consider yourself a student. Nevertheless, when you come through it, you become the teacher.

Some years ago, I realized that I needed to improve my physical health as age was creeping up on me. I was putting on more weight than I needed due to a diet of fast food every evening after work and ministry activities. I started noticing that I was getting tired easily and short-winded after I would share God's Word during Sunday worship and midweek Bible study. If I was doing simple house chores like mowing the lawn or washing the car, as soon as I was completed, I would have to take a nap. Something inside me knew that I had to make a drastic lifestyle change. I immediately made the decision to get my health back on track.

After reviewing and evaluating many health and exercise programs to find the one that was right for me, I came across one that was perfect. It had everything I needed. It consisted of a balanced meal plan, cardio workouts, and weight training. The best thing about this program was that I didn't have to have a gym membership, and I would be able to do everything right from the comfort of my own home.

Once I started the workouts, the pain that I experienced was excruciating. Everything hurt to the max; I limped when walking and couldn't move without moaning. Even at night while lying in bed, if I moved even ever so slightly, the pain would wake me up. I didn't realize how out of shape I had become. Needless to say, the first two to three weeks of this program were no fun at all. I felt as though I had more pain than progress, and I was thinking about requesting a full refund. But there was something in my spirit that kept pushing me to fight through the pain. I never gave up and kept working hard at it because I had a vision of what I wanted to see.

After about six weeks, I began to notice that the pain was not as severe, and my body was developing and starting to take shape as I had originally envisioned. Next, I began to add more resistance to my training program so that my muscles would become more defined. The more resistance I took on, the stronger and more defined my body became. The key for me was that I had to change my perspective of how I viewed the pain and stay focused on the purpose as to why I was doing it. I was on a personal assignment to ensure I would be at my best for God, my family, and myself. A long, healthy life became a priority.

What I'm telling you is that whatever afflictions you're faced with now may seem like they're designed to break you. Sometimes it's difficult to focus on the end result when all you're feeling is the resistance and struggle. But remember, the affliction is really designed to build you. You must have a disciplined drive in order to see what you believe! Whatever it takes to get through this, we must not give up.

1 Thessalonians says,

 Rejoice always, pray continually, give thanks in all circumstances; for this is God's will for you in Christ Jesus.

— 1 Thessalonians 5:16–18 (NIV)

Did you hear what Paul just said? He instructed us to "give thanks in all circumstances." The reason we can give thanks is because we already have overwhelming victory! There's that perspective again. This affliction that has entered my life can't take me out or destroy what God is doing through me. As a matter of fact, I'm praising God because I survived some things that the enemy thought would take me out.

Beloved, right here is a good place to lift your hands and release a shout of praise, because if you're reading this, it means you made it through the affliction! Change that perspective.

Let's look at what King David pens in one of his prayers to God while he is personally going through a tough time in his own life. In Psalm 34, David says,

 Many are the afflictions of the righteous, but the Lord delivers him out of them all.

— PSALM 34:19 (KJV)

There's a lot that we can learn from King David's approach toward the afflictions and trials that he was struggling with at the time he composed these powerful words. I'm sure it's something we can all relate to in some way.

At this particular point in David's life, he is an outcast and refugee who is on the run from a hostile king. We see this anointed man of God, with an assured destiny for his life, a man who knows his assignment and purpose, in a place where he's identified an affliction, and this particular affliction is rejection. Even in what he's going through, he recognizes that he is not exempt from trouble; however, he has so much confidence and trust in the God with whom he is in a covenant relationship that he knows God will rescue him from every affliction that comes his way.

It's important to recognize that David declares that the righteous will have to deal with afflictions. You and I will have situations and circumstances that will occur at different seasons in our lives. What I have learned is that we are not affliction-resistant but affliction-resilient. All I'm simply saying is that we are survivors.

Afflictions will occur because the Word of God gives us insight into them, but the good news is that they won't take us out. God will deliver us from them all. Notice that David doesn't say that my intellect, gifts, talents, family, friends, or career will deliver me. The confidence that David displays for us is clear in his faith language. David knows that afflictions will come, but he also knows that no affliction is greater than our God. He understands how much God loves him and desires the best for him.

Let's look at it this way: had it not been for the challenges against us, we would miss the champion within us. There have been some things that we were up against that should have shut us down, canceled our future, destroyed our dreams, and hindered our progress. It could have been a relationship gone bad, a firing from a job, a nasty divorce, or just being mishandled by another person or someone close to us. Whatever the situation may have been, I'm here to encourage you that *God is able* to deliver (recover, rescue, save) you out of them all.

There's nothing you can think of that God can't deliver you from. Even though we know that the righteous will have to go through trials in life, and in Psalm 34:19 David uses the word "many," which means you can have more than one struggle going on at a time, there is a great deal of comfort in knowing that our God is able to deliver us out of them all. This means that God is working and strengthening us, even when we are faced with feelings of being overwhelmed by the weight of whatever the affliction is.

God has a plan for us, and that plan is a promise of good and not evil. Jeremiah 29:11 says,

 For I know the plans I have for you," declares the Lord, "plans to prosper you and not to harm you, plans to give you hope and a future.

— JEREMIAH 29:11 (NLT)

If God says there are plans that have been tailor-cut for our lives, then we can rest in knowing we have a tomorrow.

Don't let the enemy, or anyone, put you in the position where you begin to believe that what you are struggling with is going to destroy you. Be confident that God is molding and forming you into what God has assigned you to be. God says you have a hope and a future, so believe God and deny the negative thoughts that the enemy is trying to introduce into your life.

You have an incredible future in front of you, and it has God's DNA all over it. Shout it out now:

> *I win because God has placed His prophetic Word*
> *of life over me and my entire family.*

The apostle Paul has a message he wants to relay to us, as well. The Word of God in Romans says,

 For I consider that the sufferings of this present time are not worth comparing with the glory that is to be revealed to us.

— ROMANS 8:18 (ESV)

From this powerful passage, we see that the apostle Paul is conversing about our life and the sufferings (afflictions) we will encounter in this life, not just because of our faith in God or because we have claimed to be believers, but because of basic life in this world that was broken due to sin. We know troubles will come; however, Paul wants to keep us focused on the other side of the suffering and not the suffering itself. We can rest in knowing that there is glory on the other side of the affliction that I am currently dealing with. I also know that afflictions come to stretch our faith so that we are able to endure what we are going through and not give up at the first signs of trouble.

We can call ourselves soldiers and claim we're in spiritual warfare, but we become afraid to fight or go through the warring process, even if that means to stand still and see God's salvation in it. Please note: we don't GO through; we GROW through. It is a word from Paul to encourage you and me to keep moving forward with a goal-driven tenacity even in the midst of affliction. We can't allow anything to derail or distract us; we have a determination to accomplish the goals that God has ordained for our lives. I will give birth to every assignment that God has placed in my hands. I will not be shaken or moved. *This assignment will be completed.*

Now that you've read this chapter, take time to sit with what God has revealed. This is your time to connect what you've read to where you are, and where God is leading you next. Use the following page to reflect, write, and respond.

REFLECTION

1. Which current affliction has been shaping my character?

_____

_____

_____

_____

2. What victory has God already promised me in His Word?

_____

_____

_____

_____

3. What lesson might be "waiting to be awakened" in me?

_____

_____

_____

_____

ACTION

Identify the area of struggle you're facing and consider how God is using it to shape your endurance, character, and hope (Romans 5:3–5). Talk about one of those lessons with a trusted friend or mentor.

DECLARATION

Say this declaration with conviction. Let it remind you who you are and what God has called you to do.

I'm not affliction-resistant; I'm affliction-resilient.
God delivers me out of them all.

Chapter 2

Perception

> My sheep hear my voice, and I know them, and they follow me.
>
> — John 10:27

Perception is defined as the ability to see, hear, or become aware of something through our senses. Whenever we are going through struggles and trials of any magnitude, it is crucial to stay focused on the larger picture, and that larger picture is what we are about to learn from this experience. There's always a lesson in every challenge. Far too often, when we find ourselves faced with these tough moments, we have a tendency to give all of our attention to the struggle or challenge, and then we miss the larger context of what God is trying to accomplish in us while we are navigating our way through.

Early in my corporate career and ministry, I was faced with times where the weight of the problem seemed so heavy that I felt as though it was an assignment designed specifically to destroy me before I could get a solid foundation under me. This mindset caused me to be self-absorbed and always searching for a pity party or to find others who were dealing with some of the same things so I had a shoulder to cry on. There were feelings of hurt and discouragement, which easily became a solid foundation in that particular season.

However, the real problem was that I couldn't see the bigger picture—the planned outcome. God says in Psalms,

 The Lord directs the steps of the godly. He delights in every detail of their lives. Though they stumble, they will never fall, for the Lord holds them by the hand.

— PSALM 37:23-24 (NLT)

When you let this Word from God grasp the volume of your whole heart, it causes us to change the way we see our struggles. If God says He knows the plans, that means my life is strategic. God is going to use me for His glory. There is a feeling of expectation that the end result of this will be greater than my starting point. And even more importantly, I'm protected because I'm a part of God's plan. This is what gives us hope. Just know that it's always going to work out for my good.

I remember as a little boy, I was afraid of thunderstorms. I would be outside playing on a hot summer day, but as the late afternoon would start to come in, you could feel in the atmosphere that a storm was brewing on the horizon. At this point, I would stop any summertime fun I was having with my friends and head home. Once I got in the house, I would immediately go to my room and force myself to go to sleep so I wouldn't have to endure the sight and sounds of the lightning flashing and the rumblings of the thunder that would literally shake the house. A thunderstorm to me was a terrifying moment that I didn't want to have anything to do with. Even though I knew I was safe in my own bedroom and had the protection of my parents, my perception was that storms were too much for me to handle.

One day, I decided that I was no longer going to be afraid of storms. There was a choice made that I was going to ride the next storm out. The next major storm came—you could smell the rain in the air, dark clouds started to roll in, and, in the distance, I could see the lightning flashing. This was my hour to fight against my senses that had driven this fear in me for so long. When I walked in the front door of the house, I walked into the kitchen and sat in the chair closest to the window and got comfortable. Going to my room for cover was not an option today. It was time to face the fear.

This storm to me was unlike any other; to me it was a Category 5 hurricane and an F1 tornado all wrapped up into one. That was my perception. I made it bigger than it was. How many times have we perceived our circumstances to be bigger than the promises of hope and an expected end that God has given us? The verse speaks of expected wins. I sat there and watched the entire storm from beginning to end, until the storm clouds began to move away and I could see the beautiful sunlight breaking through. It was such a proud moment for me. The creative beauty of God was seen during the storm. The gray and dark clouds were just a different shade of color; the wind was changing the shape of the trees by removing some branches; fallen leaves scattered across the landscape changed the view; and the rain made the atmosphere seem so much clearer, and a great sense of peace had settled all around, with the birds starting to sing again.

My perception was changed immediately as it related to storms. The fear of storms that had been plaguing me for years was gone instantly. All that needed to be done was to put my faith over my fear. The perception of how storms were viewed by me had shifted. I now love watching storms and even being outside in them. We have to learn how not to allow the storms in life to put a fear in our hearts that paralyzes us or prevents us from seeing the plan of God in our lives. So often we become stuck because of fear. Negative thoughts take hold over positive ones. Changing your perception or point of view will greatly increase your ability to learn the lesson in every storm.

I'm reminded of the narrative when Jesus insisted that His disciples get into the boat and cross over to the other side while He sent the people they had been ministering to that day away. After the people were sent home, Jesus went into the mountain to pray. While the disciples were on their journey to the other side of the lake, a ferocious storm—unlike what they were accustomed to—quickly arose, with harsh winds and powerful waves that tossed their boat with ease. They were in a dark place because there was no natural light out on the water due to the storm, so their perception was not clear. But their flesh could sense the effects of the danger that seemed to be all around them. I'm sure they thought they would not make it to the other side, even though Jesus had given them a Word that He would meet them there.

Then, when it seemed that all hope was lost, here came Jesus walking to them on the water, and He joined them in the storm. This is a place where we can lift our hands and give God praise! He is able to meet us in the storm because He knows the plan and purpose of the storm. But when you know that your assignment is greater than the affliction or storm you're faced with, you can handle it because He's with me in it, and we're confident God will bring us out of it.

As the disciples continued to battle the storm, they saw what they perceived to be a ghost or a spirit coming to them on the water, and again their senses caused their hearts to be gripped with fear. Jesus, knowing that they were afraid, spoke to them at once and told them, "Don't be afraid; take courage." This is another Word from Jesus that lets them know it's going to be all right. Notice, Jesus didn't wait until the storm had ceased; He spoke to them in the storm. There may be times that God will not say anything until you are in the midst of the struggle. The purpose of this is to allow you an opportunity to grow and develop your faith while giving you a new revelation as to who He is in your life.

The disciples' assignment was to go to the other side. While on their way, there were some lessons learned that changed their perception of Jesus and drew them into a deeper understanding of their relationship with Him. I want to bring out three lessons that they learned in the storm. First, they were able to see the *presence* of Jesus in the storm. Hebrews 13:5 says,

I will never fail you. I will never abandon you.

— Hebrews 13:5 (NLT)

It doesn't matter what you are going through in life or how tough it may seem; God is with us at all times, giving us the strength we need to accomplish His will. Sometimes we have to endure some hardships, but perseverance will always allow us to see the other side of the storm.

The second lesson for the disciples was the *protection* that Jesus provided to them in the midst of the storm. Once Jesus said that He would meet them on the other side, that settled it. Nothing was going to take them out or take them under. Their lives were completely secured in the direction that was spoken to them. I'm so glad that when God has an assignment for our lives—whether it be ministry, the marketplace, or assigned missions—no one can stop or hinder you if you just keep advancing faith forward and trusting God's Word over the enemy's words of defeat and destruction.

The third lesson that they learned was the *power* of Jesus in the storm. Jesus came walking on the water, and when Peter recognized who He was, he asked for permission to step out on the water with Him. Once permission was granted to come, he left everyone else behind in the boat, and he stepped out on the Word of Jesus. Notice, Peter didn't wait for anyone else to step out, nor did he allow their hesitation to deter him. God is looking for more people who will think outside of the normal confines of compromise and create moments of victory by not being bound to one way of thinking or operating. We now see Peter walking on something that he wasn't designed to walk on. Because the assignments that are given to us are so important, God will change the very nature of the thing so that what needs to be completed will get completed.

While Peter was walking on the water, he began to focus on the storm more than Jesus, which caused him to begin sinking. The joy in this story is that even when you feel like you're sinking and that you can't go on, or you become distracted by everything that's going on around you, Jesus will lift you up and bring you to safety. Jesus helped Peter back into the boat, and when they were all in the boat, the storm ceased and the lake was still. And notice this: they all went to the other side, as Jesus said.

Know that there's an assignment that God has for you to do. And if you get discouraged along the way, keep confidence in the Presence, Protection, and Power of God. What will give you confidence is when you change your perception. See every problem as a puzzle waiting to be solved. Know that God has given you all the pieces to put things in order. Just have patience and move confidently through the process. Initiate a solution to whatever it is. There's always an answer. Pray and ask God for wisdom and direction. Also, don't get overwhelmed; believe you are able to overcome whatever it is that seems too much of a heavy burden. Finally, distance yourself from the distractions so that your focus is clearer. It's important to withdraw from the things and, in some cases, people who will not add any value to the situation at hand. There are some afflictions we allow to enter into our lives that we could have said no to from the very beginning. Remember, change your perception; see the expected end that God promised you.

Now that you've read this chapter, take time to sit with what God has revealed. This is your time to connect what you've read to where you are, and where God is leading you next. Use the following page to reflect, write, and respond.

REFLECTION

1. Where have I magnified the storm over the Savior?

_____

_____

_____

_____

2. What would change if I saw this problem as a solvable puzzle?

_____

_____

_____

_____

3. Which distractions need distance so I can see clearly?

_____

_____

_____

_____

ACTION

Transform fear into faith in real time. When fear arises, pause and declare a statement of faith in its place. Keep your heart fixed on the outcome God has ordained, trusting Him to bring it to completion.

DECLARATION

Say this declaration with conviction. Let it remind you who you are and what God has called you to do.

I choose God's perspective.
My eyes are on the promise, not the problem.

CHAPTER 3

ENCOURAGEMENT

But David encouraged himself in the Lord his God.

— 1 SAMUEL 30:6 (KJV)

S atan is well aware that discouragement can destroy our passion to fulfill purpose. It quickly begins to strip us of our desire to execute every God-given assignment. This is one of the tools that the enemy of our soul will use against us to keep us stuck at a certain place in life. Discouragement will show up in many forms and can quickly find its way into our lives through the things we hear with our ears, perceive with our eyes, and imagine with our minds. It could simply be a word from a mother who said too much or a father who just didn't say enough.

Another pathway through which discouragement can enter our lives is through relationships that seem to show signs of a promising future, only to end up leaving us brokenhearted and alone, while desperately searching for someone or something to fill the void. In addition, it could be a career moment when it seemed as though things were finally headed in the right direction. Your dreams and aspirations may be falling into place, but, in reality, there may be some unmet expectations that once again left you emotionally frustrated, confused, and ready to throw in the towel.

So, the question is: *what can we do when we find ourselves in an empty place without any hope or courage to pursue forward?* This place is called discouragement. It's that time in our life when, at some point, we feel that there is a void that needs to be filled. We are all well aware that we have a heavenly Father who is always there for us, and we are confident that He is able to bring us out of this place of discouragement. But in spite of that, we can still find ourselves being held hostage there. May I suggest to you that even in this state of mind, we have to actively participate in the process of our own escape. Yes, we know that it takes a level of faith and courage to move forward, but as James states,

 What good is it, dear brothers and sisters, if you say you have faith but don't show it by your actions? Can that kind of faith save anyone?

— JAMES 2:14 (NLT)

In other words, faith without a corresponding action will not always produce the results we are looking for. For example, you can't pray and ask God for a job while, at the same time, you sit at home relaxing, not doing anything to job-search or send out résumés. If you take that approach, you will be jobless longer than you planned to be.

There are steps that go along with your prayers and faith walk. You must take the appropriate actions in order to have forward progression. You have to start thinking positive, conduct the comprehensive job search, send out multiple résumés, take time to prepare for the interview, and put all the right disciplines in place so that you are ready to begin the new career when it arrives. This is the place where we all could use a little bit of encouragement to become active in our approach to success.

Encouragement is such a vital element for all of us because it helps us to continue moving forward with complete confidence in our

God-given assignments, even when trouble is evident on every side. Too many times, we will wait for someone to come and tell us we are doing well, or we enter a place where we need their accolades in order to feel like we are successful. The truth of the matter is we shouldn't rely so much on the opinions of others in order to be encouraged.

The real key is this: if there is no one to encourage you, God has given you the ability to dig deep down and encourage yourself. My friend, you have the ability to speak and/or think yourself right out of any negative situations or circumstances because God is at work within us. Ephesians 3 says,

 Now all glory to God, who is able, through His mighty power at work within us, to accomplish infinitely more than we might ask or think.

— EPHESIANS 3:20 (NLT)

Because God is able, that means we are able—able to overcome every attack against us that would keep us from completing and fulfilling the assigned purposes of our very being.

A powerful narrative about self-encouragement is found in the 30th chapter of 1 Samuel. I love reading this narrative about David and the moment he suffered at Ziklag. Here we find David, the future king of Israel, in a season of adversity, a place where direction seems distant. He's caught between two extremes. No longer is he in his father Jesse's house, and he's not in the palace as king yet. There are assassination attempts on his life by King Saul. Because of this, David is a fugitive and finds himself in exile living among the Philistines, along with his men and their families. They are hiding out in a town called Ziklag.

On this particular occasion, David and his men were returning home from a battle. They were all extremely tired, and, as you would expect, everyone was excited to see their families and friends once again. As they approached Ziklag, they noticed that their town had been ravaged by the Amalekites. The Amalekites invaded the city, burned their homes to the ground, and kidnapped their women and children. What David and his men were witnessing was beyond comprehension, and this caused them to experience agonizing grief. Each man, including David, began to weep uncontrollably. To add even more weight to an already disturbing situation, his men began to blame David for this calamity that had happened to them.

Conversations began to swirl among his men that if David had not taken them into battle, they would not be in this predicament. When our lives are faced with adversity and afflictions, you will discover that it's human nature to try to find blame even when it's not warranted. When things oftentimes do not go according to plan, we have a tendency to blame ourselves or someone else for the failure. The key to overcoming this emotional setback is to see the problem as a puzzle needing to be solved.

Many times, I have personally turned my struggles into some sort of game, quickly finding ways and different strategies to win, while at the same time giving God praise for the opportunity to use the gifts and talents that He has given me. This kind of mindset will always give birth to a winning determination with creative solutions.

Reflecting on this narrative, I can imagine David's 600 men weeping and grieving as though their hopes and dreams of a prosperous future had been shattered. In addition, they were probably using some choice words while blaming David for all that had happened to them. And to top it all off, there was a stirring up inside them—such rage and pain—that they were now talking about stoning him to death. I am certain David didn't see any of this coming.

Here we now find David being faced with an overwhelming affliction. King Saul wants him dead; he is a fugitive on the run; their homes have been burned to the ground; their families have been kidnapped by their enemies; and now there's rebellion against him in his own camp. How can it get any worse? It is at this point that David does something that is amazing to me. The Bible says that David encouraged himself in the Lord his God. Other translations say that he "strengthened himself." May I suggest to you that a crisis situation will always bring out the best in us. When I think of this moment in his life, David is probably sitting in the dust with tears streaming down his face while confidently praying and seeking God for direction.

As he has done in the past, he begins to softly sing a song of worship to the Lord. Because of his relationship and trust in God, he will not allow himself to fall into depression or hopelessness. There is also another important point here that we need to highlight and recognize.

Did you notice that David did not blame or complain to God when he was experiencing this calamity? Becoming defensive and allowing the words of rebellion from his men to penetrate his heart was not an option. He knows that he is *built to win.* It's David's attitude during a time of affliction that causes him not to die in this place.

Your attitude will always determine your altitude. My friend, you have to wake up every day with a winning attitude. For David, it was imperative that he find the place where the presence of God was. He needed to get into a place that was above his problem. Being in God's presence is a necessity for him to be able to accomplish his life's assignment. I think this is a valuable lesson for all of us. When we are going through a rough season, that's not the time to run away from God, but to run to Him. David does three key things that lift him out of this pit of despair and place him back on the right track.

The first thing we see him do is to put his feelings in check. May I suggest to you that if we don't control our emotions, our emotions will control us? We see here how he was able to encourage himself in the Lord. Whenever our emotions are out of control, we oftentimes will not make wise and rational decisions. When we are emotionally driven, it becomes difficult to make the best decision that will allow us to resolve a crisis situation. Instead, we look for the best option or decision that we think will allow us to be put in a more favorable position as it relates to the opinions of others. We find ourselves becoming more consumed with what people think about us rather than what God thinks about us.

There will be times in life when our choices will not be praised by public opinion. But as long as we are doing what is right, you will not only add value to your own life but also to the lives of others around you. When God has an assignment for you, you will find that your enemies will do all they can to try to cause you to shift your focus. But I declare today that you will be successful in everything you do. And if you are reading this book today, it simply means you are still working toward completing the assignment that God has given you.

Life will always be full of challenging situations, but I have come to realize that what Satan can't destroy, he does his best to distract. Even as David faced so many dangerous challenges in his life, his enemies could not take him out because he had to complete his God-given assignment. And that assignment was to be the greatest king in the history of Israel.

Once David gathered his emotions and pulled himself together, it was time to move forward to identify a solution to the problem. At this point, who could he trust or confide in? All of his senses were heightened to everything that was going on around him: the sounds of agony from his troops, the smell of burning wood and cloth from the homes and tents that had been destroyed by fire, and the painful sight of an empty village that was void of any signs of life. Trying to process all of this while knowing you have to make some strategic decisions is a tough moment for anyone. That is a lot of pressure for any one person to deal with at one time. To add misery to mayhem, those closest to him have turned their backs on him, and, because of this, I'm sure David is feeling a deep sense of rejection, hurt, and betrayal.

Many of us have found ourselves in this emotional position at some point in our lives. It may not be the exact same situation that we see occurring in David's life, but it's a place where we feel isolated and void of any help or support—desperately seeking an ear to listen or a shoulder to lean on. How do we cope when it seems like everyone has walked away from us and there's not one individual responding to our cry for help? It's here where we have to fight a strong fight and turn on our faith. Being in a season of isolation can be a very dangerous spot for anyone. It's here oftentimes where negative thoughts are conceived.

The enemy will begin to lie to us and say things like, "Everyone is against you," or, "You will never recover from this." It's never a good feeling to feel like you have no one to turn to and that you're in this alone. When David finds himself in this low state, I believe he is reminded that his assurance is not in man but in the God with whom he has a loving relationship. This is where we have to pull out the résumé of our life and remember all the ways that God has already rescued us. It's here where we see David shift into his assignment while he is still in a time of affliction.

The second thing David does is he activates his faith and does what he knows best, and that is get in the presence of God. According to 1 Samuel 30:6–7 (MSG), David strengthened himself with trust in his God. He ordered Abiathar the priest, son of Ahimelech to bring him the ephod so he can consult God. Abiathar brought it to David. David now connects to the ephod, or priestly garment, that is an outward symbol of his authority as a leader, but, most importantly, it shows his connection to God. When in this season of distress, he goes to God.

He didn't quit, leave the church, tell his men that his season was up, get intoxicated, run back to old habits, or start making negative comments. Instead, he went into a space of worship and prayer to seek guidance and direction from the One who holds the future in His hands, the One who has a plan already laid out to prosper us and give us an expected end. It was important for David to bring God into his problem because he knew that God was the only one who could repair what had occurred not only in his life but in everyone's life around him.

When you know that you have been anointed for a particular life assignment, you can move with conviction knowing that the task will be fulfilled. Don't let negative thoughts or conversations distort what you know you are able to accomplish. Never downplay your gifts or abilities, or fail to speak the language of faith over yourself. You can speak into existence not just your own personal victory, but you have enough anointing on your life to speak on behalf of those around you. The Bible consistently teaches us to speak positive words into our atmosphere. Our faith words will turn your troubled situation around if you believe what you say. You have to have positive communication.

Lastly, the third thing David does is that he responded to God's response. Notice, David now asks God a question that is spoken with a language of unwavering faith and absolute certainty. Verse 8 of this same chapter says, "Then David asked the Lord, 'Should I chase after this band of raiders? Will I catch them?'" And the Lord told him, "Yes, go after them. You will surely recover everything that was taken from you." David knew he was able to take out the Amalekites, but he still wanted to do it the way God wanted it done. He is obedient to God even in his affliction. The Bible says,

> So do not throw away this confident trust in the Lord. Remember the great reward it brings you! Patient endurance is what you need now, so you will continue to do God's will. Then you will receive all that He has promised.

> — HEBREWS 10:35–36 (NLT)

When the treacherous storms are formed and enter our lives, because of the chaos they will many times bring, we can find our faith in God beginning to unravel. This is not the time to give up, but to hold on to God more than ever before. It's imperative that we seek God for patience and direction. These are the times that remind us who we are in God and who God is to us. We must lift our heads and fix our eyes on the outcome. Never take your eyes off the direction you are supposed to be going in. Just because we are going through it does not negate the promises that He made to us. In good, bad, or uncertain times, one thing that I'm sure of is that God is still able to rescue us from destruction. Even if we should slip and fall, He promises to never let go of your hand. He will lift you back up so that you can continue to move forward. Never forget that the Lord is our assurance, our rewarder, and our loving God.

David responds to God's response to his prayers. And the outcome for David was that God would give him the victory and that all would be recovered. There was nothing for him to worry about. In spite of the physical effort it would take to recover it, he didn't let this discourage him. David understood the assignment, rallied his troops, and carried it out to completion. He functioned as the leader that he was anointed to be and didn't allow the affliction to prevent him from gaining a valuable experience.

I believe even this trying event was a part of his development process to become an even greater leader. It's one thing to hear God's answer, but it's another thing to respond to it. How many times have you heard God tell you what to do, but you still remain still because you allowed the affliction to hinder the opportunity to allow it to develop you? God always has a plan for you in the middle of the process. Don't forget that the process is just preparing you for the promotion.

I am reminded of a time in my own life when I became discouraged. At seven years old, my mother signed me up for piano lessons. Never did music cross my mind as something to take seriously. However, I quickly fell in love with it, and the rest is history. I give God all the praise for my gifting in the area of music because it changed my life forever, and it was the foundation of who I am today as a corporate executive and pastor.

With this formal and disciplined training, I was reading music and playing classical piano at an early age. When I was about eleven years old, I was scheduled to perform in my very first piano recital. The memory of this moment is still pretty fresh in my mind.

Preparing for this was a major deal in the Monroe household. No matter what sports or street games we were playing outside, I would hear my mother calling my name for me to come home. Her voice seemed to echo all over the place, and the entire neighborhood heard it. The next thing I knew, everyone was yelling out, "Darrin, Mrs. Monroe is calling you." This was a time when there were no cell phones and everyone respected all adults and would use a prefix when speaking to or about them.

And now back to my story. No matter what I was doing, it stopped immediately, and I knew it was either time to eat or time for piano practice. It was a part of the Sadie Monroe regimen to practice every day after school for thirty minutes to an hour. Over and over, you would hear these same classical compositions ringing throughout the house, as I played them on the living room piano, constantly working through all the kinks and ensuring that the classical pieces being played were with precision and accuracy.

Finally, it was time for the big night. All the hard work I put in would be displayed for all to hear. I quietly sat, watched, and listened to all the other students execute their songs while determining who I had to beat and how; however, competition wasn't the point for me. After about seven or eight students, it was now my turn to turn it out. When my name was called, with sheet music in hand, I made my way to that black baby grand piano. It was my very first time sitting at one. My heart raced and my hands were sweaty, but I knew I was ready. Here's my time to show the other students how it's done. The most complicated music was at my fingertips, waiting to be shared.

As I began to play, it started off okay, but it ended up a tremendous mess. I lost my fingering, tempo, and confidence. Getting through it at that point was all I wanted to do. If I'm not mistaken, I believe I had to stop and start over a couple of times. Finally, I'm done. I hear people clapping and yelling, but I know they were just being polite and trying to keep me from collapsing from embarrassment. Of course, according to Mom, I was the best, and Stevie Wonder was backstage waiting to sign me up for his next tour. She was always my biggest fan.

But this is the point of the story: when I was finished playing, it was my peers and those whom I called my friends that really broke me. My courage at this point seemed to shatter into a thousand pieces. Some laughed on the side, while others just smirked and didn't say anything to me. I tried to play it off and make excuses for my bad performance, but they just didn't seem to care. To make matters worse, salt was added to the already opened wound, and some of the boys started talking about putting a band together, and I wasn't even asked to play a tambourine. They totally excluded and isolated me from anything past this moment. I stood there alone and confused at such an early age. Being an only child, all I wanted was to be accepted by others. I was completely devastated.

This led me to run over to my mom and just bury my broken ego in her chest. I was crying like a baby, and I think I wanted to give this piano thing up altogether. It wasn't my idea to play anyway. It was something my mom signed me up for. At this point, my mom lifted my head, gave me a positive word to let me know that I did an excellent job, and told me that I would need to keep working hard to get better. After I had shed my tears, I realized that if none of the other students wanted me around, I would fly solo and just do what I needed to do.

I have always recognized that God was with me, even at such an early age. My parents would always teach me to acknowledge God in everything I did. So when I was faced with any kind of challenge, I was confident that God would be in it with me and that He had given me the ability to work through any struggle.

With the challenge I was currently facing, if something was going to change, I would have to pray and ask God for help and lean on His direction that would be planted in my heart. Once God gives us the instruction on how to move forward, then that movement would have to be initiated by me. I would have to locate the encouragement from within.

I believe this is the first time I ever had to encourage myself to overcome a feeling of defeat. There will be many times in our lives when we will have to dig down deep and pull out just what is needed to navigate our way through the afflictions of life. This moment of ridicule and discouragement was an affliction for this eleven-year-old boy. It literally robbed me of my belief in my ability to play the piano. But, in spite of the way I was feeling, there was a determination and drive to prove everyone who was making fun of my musical performance wrong.

This desire to be the best pushed me forward. Whatever anyone had to say didn't matter anymore. No one would ever laugh at my piano performances again. I re-evaluated my approach toward greatness. I started preparing for the next recital earlier than I normally would. It was only a month after that first recital, and I was already eleven months ahead of schedule. It was not an option to allow that one moment of hurt to discourage me from any of my future musical assignments. Literally, in my mind, I could visualize each student I was going after. Yes, I was going after those who, at the time, I considered to be my enemies, and I was certain they would respect me after the next recital.

Just as God told David, I was going to recover all. On a side note: recover what, you may ask? Who knows, but I was going to recover something! This time I chose two classical pieces, "Beethoven's Fifth Symphony in C Major" and "Avalanche," and, to make it sweet, I added an R&B composition called "Best of My Love" by the Emotions. When it was time for my second recital, I knew I was on top of my game. I had prepared so much that I didn't even need the sheet music. It was now in my heart. Once I finished my flawless performance, I sat there and just stared at the keys as though I had run a marathon. At this point, the room erupted with loud applause and a standing ovation. Yes, I completed the assignment.

This time, I was asked to join the band, and all those who laughed were now saying how much they enjoyed what they had heard. It was a moment that still lives with me and encourages me to never give up but to find ways to push toward the winner's circle.

Even as I am writing this chapter, I now reflect back on this from a different set of eyes; this is now being seen through a mature set of eyes. And with that, I realize the importance of staying true to the assignments in our lives and not allowing life to distract us from destiny. I now wonder where my life would be had I allowed discouragement to cause me to give up on the gift of playing the piano. It would have been a domino effect that not only would have changed my life but also the lives of so many others. Through this gift of music, I have been able to get involved with so many wonderful things, from playing in a college choir to starting an outreach community choir called Chosen Generation, which went into the prisons and street corners spreading the Gospel of Jesus Christ, to starting a church, to meeting so many incredible people and impacting lives along the way, to even my son having a successful musical career.

All it takes is for us to allow one moment of affliction to enter our lives and rob us of the assignment that God has for us to accomplish. Always remember to encourage yourself whenever the hard moments should arise. There are so many people waiting for you to arrive because you are a part of their destiny.

* * *

Now that you've read this chapter, take time to sit with what God has revealed. This is your time to connect what you've read to where you are, and where God is leading you next. Use the following page to reflect, write, and respond.

REFLECTION

1. Where am I waiting for others to affirm what God already said?

_____

_____

_____

_____

2. What does "encourage myself in the Lord" look like for me this week?

_____

_____

_____

_____

3. Which emotions need submitting so wisdom can lead?

_____

_____

_____

_____

ACTION

Create a 3-minute "self-encouragement" routine (Scripture, worship line, prayer) and use it daily.

DECLARATION

Say this declaration with conviction. Let it remind you who you are and what God has called you to do.

> *God's power is at work within me.*
> *I encourage myself and advance.*

CHAPTER 4

DETERMINATION

> Do you not know that in a race all the runners run, but only one gets the prize? Run in such a way as to get the prize. Everyone who competes in the games goes into strict training. They do it to get a crown that will not last, but we do it to get a crown that will last forever. Therefore I do not run like someone running aimlessly; I do not fight like a boxer beating the air. No, I strike a blow to my body and make it my slave so that after I have preached to others, I myself will not be disqualified for the prize.
>
> — 1 Corinthians 9:24-27 (NIV)

As far back as I can remember, I've always been very analytical in my thought process. No matter what I was doing, it all had to make logical sense, along with involving very calculated movements. I looked at life very carefully and would plan things out in such detail that I wouldn't expect anything to go wrong. But, on the other side of that, I was an only child who many times felt alone, isolated, and awkward. However, in spite of those feelings, I was able to keep a positive attitude, with the end result and expectations always in view. I had such drive and determination in everything that I did. So, when it came to my future career ambitions and goals, I can remember literally speaking them into existence with confidence and a clear vision of the path to get there.

My first career job was in a microbiology lab located on Park Ave in Hoboken, New Jersey. I can recall preparing for my grand entrance into that laboratory. I woke up early that Monday morning, and the sun was shining brightly through my bedroom window. The butterflies in my stomach were fluttering all over the place. Feelings of being nervous and excited, all at the same time, shook me to the very core. I jumped out of bed and slipped on those navy-blue slacks with a crease that would cut you if you touched it, a starched snow-white shirt, and a bold, executive-looking tie that screamed out Wall Street executive. Oh yeah, and don't forget the chocolate-brown briefcase with the combination lock that I received as a high school graduation gift. I was so ready for business. And just know my mom ironed my clothes the night before because she knew ironing wasn't my best skill. No one could iron creases in slacks like Sadie Monroe.

I decided not to wear a blazer that day, because I was certain I would be getting my first official white lab coat. It was 7:30 a.m. and time to get moving. I hopped in the car and headed on this new life's journey. Driving to the lab, I don't even remember playing music. More than likely, I was probably talking to myself for the entire 20-minute drive. Once I got in the area of the building, I was trying desperately to locate a parking space so I wouldn't be late. The thought of being late on the first day just added to my already elevated anxiety. I found a place to park, and I was doing great with time. I jumped out of the car and ran to the front door of the United States Testing Co. Here I was, now standing in front of my destiny and dream job. I remember looking up at the name of the company and saying, "Monroe, let's make it happen."

Walking up the stairs with my back straight and head up, I went through the front entrance and found myself standing at the reception desk. With a confident yet nervous voice, I said, "My name is

Darrin Monroe, and I'm a new employee, and I'm here for the biological sciences division." She politely told me to sign in and have a seat; she would let them know I was here. Then it went to the next level: she announced to the executive administrator of biological sciences that Mr. Darrin Monroe had arrived. Hearing someone announce my name with the prefix "Mr." was totally unexpected, and the sound was so sweet to my ears. The smile on my face made the muscles in my jaw hurt. It was difficult not to show my excitement and, at the same time, keep a professional disposition about myself.

The receptionist told me to take the elevator to the fifth floor and that they were expecting me. I walked quickly into the elevator and proceeded to the fifth floor. When the elevator stopped, the door slowly opened. Here I am, starting a new chapter in my life. With a swag in my step and a slight taste of arrogance in my mouth, I opened the door that said Microbiological Lab, walked into the lab, and, with great articulation, introduced myself to my new manager. I was now ready to solve all the biological issues in the world.

I knew God had orchestrated this moment and blessed me with this job, and there was no doubt in my mind about that. At the time, this was my dream job, and to top it all off, I was in my senior year of college. I didn't have my degree yet, and I was already gracing the career field I dreamed about. I was on top of the world and in complete awe. My manager looked at me with a smile and welcomed me to this new world of wonder and science. Her next statement to me was, "Let me show you around and introduce you to the others."

This was the moment I had been waiting for. Would I be shown *Escherichia coli* or some other organism that I had studied in microbiology class? Would I be given the task of isolating some mystery growth so that I could do a gram stain for identification and classification? Would I get the chance to name this new organism after me? A name was already picked out in my mind. My discovery and organism would be identified as Darrin:0321. The thoughts were spinning in my mind. My heart was racing and pounding in my chest. This was my time to shine and show my parents that their only son was doing what he had told them would be done.

The lab was absolutely beautiful, a scientific marvel in my eyes. Glassware everywhere, a pristine environment with sterile clean rooms, machines making the sounds of analytical data production, and the smell of chemical solutions in the atmosphere. If it were today's time, this moment would have been on Facebook Live and selfies taken for sure. As this introductory tour was coming to an end, surely there had to be more. I didn't see the moment I was expecting. Where was the lab coat, desk, and my first microbiological problem to solve that would change the world of science as we know it? Oh yeah, that's right; surely you always save the best for last.

Then, she introduced me to the area where I would be working. Yes, the end of the tour, the place of my destiny in this new season. And as we turned the corner, the very last stop of the tour was my office—and it was the test tube washing area. She informed me that their dishwasher was broken, and they needed someone to wash test tubes to help them catch up. All around this room were stacks and stacks of dirty test tubes. They were literally stacked from the countertop up to the ceiling. There had to be at least a thousand dirty test tubes just waiting to be cleaned.

The mere sight of it was discouraging and incredibly overwhelming to look at. It was difficult to even process how I was going to accomplish this task. This moment literally clouded my vision, and the excitement had turned to disappointment. This wasn't what I had originally signed up for. Then reality really began to set in, and instead of the pristine white lab coat I had been dreaming about for the past two weeks, she handed me an apron so I wouldn't get my starched white shirt dirty. To add to my shock, she handed me a pipe cleaner. It was a little thin wire with bristles on the end. This was my cleaning equipment to make sure a thousand test tubes were cleaned to the level that they could be reused.

Slowly and with much hesitation, I rolled up my sleeves, loosened my tie, grabbed that pipe cleaner, and went to work. And one by one, I started washing test tubes. Even though there was a slight feeling of discouragement, I couldn't allow my current situation to dictate the final outcome. There was a feeling of determination that rose up within me that gave me the strength to push past the immediate moment. The realization was that there is always a lesson to be learned during the process. God was actually preparing me for a destination that far exceeded my expectation. We know God always has a plan for our lives, but He doesn't always give us the details of how we will arrive.

The truth of the matter is, if we knew the steps within the process, many of us would give up during the process because of the endurance that is required to make it. There were moments when it was difficult to see through all the soap suds and water. All that really crossed my mind was, how was I going to tell my family and friends that I was a test tube washer? How would this skill look on my future résumé? However, God had a much bigger plan for my life. He was humbling me and, at the same time, developing me for greater— greater not just in a professional career but also within ministry.

I look back at it now and can say it was all a setup for more. As I have matured over the years, there is a greater understanding of what Paul says,

 In everything give thanks: for this is the will of God in Christ Jesus concerning you.

— 1 THESSALONIANS 5:18 (KJV)

This is because God is always positioning us for unlimited winning moments. Focusing on my current dilemma would not lead me to the win, but I began to focus on the opportunity of what I could become. This was now the goal, trusting that God was working this out for my good.

What was once a challenging situation has now transformed me into a determined individual who would allow God to order the direction of this season. And yes, I say season, because it wasn't going to be permanent. God was teaching me a level of determination that allows one to see every struggle from a different perspective. It's important that you stay focused on the desired outcome.

My determination for success disciplined me. Managing my emotions and not allowing my emotions to manage me was necessary for my growth. There was no one reporting to me, so the lesson learned was that you must move things forward in order to see the assignments that God has assigned to us successfully completed—and there will be times when you will have to go alone. There will not be anyone on the sidelines cheering you on or helping to bear the weight of the load. I worked hard day after day and week after week cleaning tubes with no outside support.

There was a very important concept for me to grasp, because God knew—even if I didn't at the time—that He had a pastoral calling in my future. And this was a part of the wilderness training to prepare me for it. He had to know I would remain consistent even in unfavorable situations. He knew there would be times in which I would have to serve and work alone. The assignment would have to be executed even when there was no one to help or to call upon. There was tremendous purpose in this entire journey, and as it became clearer, I became more excited about the possibilities.

I cleaned test tubes for about three months, and I was determined to be the best test tube washer there ever was. I came to work with ambition and a plan to do everything with a spirit of excellence. I never complained and always kept a positive attitude. I kept my emotions in complete check because I refused to allow them to pull me out of my character. There were days when I felt like this was a waste of time and that there had to be a better way, but my spirit wouldn't let me leave. Each day I entered the lab, I was thankful for a job.

When we allow ourselves to get distracted and discouraged, it distances us from the desired destination. Every day I began to tell myself that I was supposed to be here. If this truth were not so, God wouldn't have placed me in this position. So many times, when we ask God for something, we want the promise but never the process. But it's going through the process that brings out the best performance in each and every one of us. The process gives us the experience of how to handle the hills and valleys that come with life. And every time we conquer a battle, it builds our determination in such a way that our faith and hope are increased.

Always give God thanks and praise for the process. It's here we mature, build, and sharpen our giftings. What I thought was a valley experience was really God allowing me to identify what He planted inside of me. I love the way the Amplified Bible translation puts Philippians:

> I can do all things [which He has called me to do] through Him who strengthens and empowers me [to fulfill His purpose—I am self-sufficient in Christ's sufficiency; I am ready for anything and equal to anything through Him who infuses me with inner strength and confident peace.
>
> — PHILIPPIANS 4:13 (AMP)

"All things" means that everything is attainable and achievable for me when it fulfills His will for our lives. There is always a promising path to every promotion in life; we just have to learn how to be patient while God is preparing the path. Proverbs 3:5–6 reminds us:

> Trust in and rely confidently on the Lord with all your heart, and do not rely on your own insight or understanding; in all your ways know and acknowledge and recognize Him, and He will make your paths straight and smooth [removing obstacles that block your way].
>
> — PROVERBS 3:5–6 (AMP)

The Lord reminded me that I asked for a job in a microbiology lab and that I wanted to become a microbiologist. Staying focused on what you know God has put in your heart to do takes determination. Our enemy, Satan, will always try to do what he can to break your will and introduce distractions into your life to move you away from your assignment. He knows that when you recognize divine destiny, there is a level of determination that will give you the strength to keep pushing that assignment forward to completion.

Another great example of determination is found in Acts, the 14th chapter. Here we find Paul and Barnabas fulfilling the calling and assignments over their lives. They had been preaching and teaching the Gospel of Jesus Christ so effectively that both Jews and Gentiles were giving their hearts to Jesus. God also proved that the message they preached was true by allowing them the ability to perform miracles, signs, and wonders. However, the Jews were still able to rally together a mob to rebel against everything that Paul and Barnabas were doing. The mob stoned the apostle Paul, dragged his body out of the city, and left him for dead.

However, something amazing happens in Acts:

 But as the believers gathered around him, he got up and went back into the town.

— Acts 14:20 (NLT)

I believe that Paul clearly understood that his assignment was greater than his present affliction, and it was his determination to do the will of his Father that gave him the strength he needed to rise up and continue the assignment.

You see, when the passion we have to fulfill purpose is released, it will give you the power to push through the pain—especially when you know that there is a Word of protection and provision over your life.

How many times have you found yourself in situations where you are supporting others during their lowest moments, and yet you are still met with rejection and opposition that shakes the very core of your being? Note that whenever you're doing something great for God, you are not exempt from opposition, persecution, or suffering.

Listen to the words of the apostle Paul to his spiritual son Timothy.

> But you, Timothy, certainly know what I teach, and how
> I live, and what my purpose in life is. You know my
> faith, my patience, my love, and my endurance. You
> know how much persecution and suffering I have
> endured. You know all about how I was persecuted in
> Antioch, Iconium, and Lystra—but the Lord rescued me
> from all of it. Yes, and everyone who wants to live a
> godly life in Christ Jesus will suffer persecution.
>
> — Timothy 3:10–12 (NLT)

My friends, the attacks will come your way to try to get you to give up on the vision, dream, or goal that God has placed in your heart. This is the time when I need you to have the determination to fight through this temporary circumstance. There are three things you need to do:

1. Remain obedient to the assignment. The power of the Holy Spirit will give you everything you need to survive this season. Don't walk away just because things get hard. Know that if God has called you to do it, He's already given you everything you need to fulfill it. You have the DNA of a winner all over you, and nothing can stop you but you!

2. Recognize the opportunity of opposition. You have to go through it in order to get to it! There is always an opportunity to be discovered in opposition. Determination says fight until you have success in your hands. Don't quit too early, because you will miss the opportunity and the valuable lessons that come with it. Paul saw an opportunity to impact lives, and he was determined to bring it to completion. Determination made him unstoppable. Yes, as Paul was, so are you! *You are unstoppable!*

3. Remove all obstacles. The pain will change when you change.

Get rid of the people, places, and things that are causing you pain and discomfort. When a person has a pain in their body, if you do nothing about it, the pain will persist. It's not until you address it that you can come up with a plan to take care of it in such a way that it no longer hinders your progress. Be determined to press toward your purpose. Don't lose your *determination*.

* * *

Now that you've read this chapter, take time to sit with what God has revealed. This is your time to connect what you've read to where you are, and where God is leading you next. Use the following page to reflect, write, and respond.

REFLECTION

1. What "test tube" task is training my character right now?

_____

_____

_____

_____

2. Where do I need discipline more than motivation?

_____

_____

_____

_____

3. Which expectations do I need to surrender to embrace God's process?

_____

_____

_____

_____

ACTION

Pick one difficult responsibility. Define a simple excellence standard and meet it five days in a row.

DECLARATION

Say this declaration with conviction. Let it remind you who you are and what God has called you to do.

I am disciplined, diligent, and determined.
Process is producing promotion.

CHAPTER 5

PERSERVERANCE

> Blessed is the one who perseveres under trial because, having stood the test, that person will receive the crown of life that the Lord has promised to those who love him.
>
> — JAMES 1:12 (NIV)

Sunday, March 22, 2020, is a day that will forever be etched into the very fabric of my mind. It was the beginning of the COVID-19 pandemic, and the world as we knew it was changing right before our very eyes. There was so much uncertainty about what this virus was all about. Fear, anxiety, and panic began to grip the hearts of everyone you spoke to. This was the only topic the television news stations were covering, and everyone on social media had something to report about how it was affecting them or someone they knew.

This was also the Sunday that our leadership decided to have everyone stay home except for the essential people who were needed to livestream the morning worship experience. These individuals included my wife and me, the praise team singers, musicians, and the media team. Despite what was going on in the world, we all felt very confident that this would be the only Sunday we would have to do this, because in our lifetimes we had always seen America bounce back pretty quickly from crisis situations.

After the worship service was over, we all hugged and talked for a few moments at the back of the sanctuary. It was a very somber moment. Each one of us shared our thoughts on the situation and expressed our concerns along with our confidence. Looking back on this moment now, we had no idea that it would be close to a year before we would actually be in each other's physical presence again. And for sure, we couldn't have imagined the journey that each one of us was about to experience.

We locked up the church, gave some hugs, and stated with a smile that we would probably see each other next week. My wife and I proceeded to our vehicle and began driving home. We had only been driving for about 20 minutes when we got a call from one of our musicians. He was very upset, and you could hear the distress in his voice. He said, "I had to rush my mom to the hospital, and she's having a difficult time breathing. Please pray, because they wouldn't let me enter the hospital with her. I had to drop her off at the emergency room and leave."

I immediately prayed with him and assured him that his mom would be okay and that she would be home before he knew it. He calmed down a little, thanked me for the prayer, and promised to give an update when he heard something.

My wife and I finally made it home, and as we always did after a worship service, we changed our clothes and were getting ready to grab a bite to eat. Then all of a sudden, my phone started ringing again, and this time I saw it was my son Aaron. I answered with my normal, "What's up, A-Rock? " I immediately sensed in his voice that something was wrong. He then told me that he had found my dad sitting on the kitchen floor, not feeling well. I instructed my son to call 911 to get him some help and told him I was on my way.

I tried to talk to my dad on the phone, but he was really out of it and didn't want to speak with me. I dropped everything I was doing and made my way to my dad's house to further assess the situation. While I was driving, I had a personal prayer session in the car, praying every prayer I could possibly think of. I had no idea what to expect. As I got closer to my father's home, my heart was beating out of my chest, and all kinds of thoughts were racing through my mind. However, the Holy Spirit brought me a calming peace that gave me confidence that everything would be okay.

As I continued talking to God, I told Him that I believed He had everything under control and that I needed Him to step into this situation. As I turned the corner of the street where my dad lived, the first thing I saw was the ambulance sitting in the driveway. I quickly pulled my car into the closest spot I could find and parked the best way I could, not caring if the car was blocking any of the neighbors' driveways.

I jumped out of my car quickly and ran up the stairs into his house, missing every other stair. Walking into the kitchen, I saw my dad sitting in a chair with the paramedics attending to him. They told me they had taken all of his vitals and everything seemed okay. However, because of the growing number of cases due to the COVID outbreak and my dad being 84 years old, they thought he would be safer at home rather than being transported to the hospital, where the risks were much greater for being infected with the virus. I totally agreed with them and stated I would take him to his doctor for a follow-up first thing in the morning.

The paramedics packed up their equipment, wished us the best, and headed to their next call. After personally evaluating my dad's condition, I noticed that he was unable to walk five feet without becoming extremely out of breath. He was exhausted and hadn't eaten at all that day. This was completely out of the ordinary for him. This is a man who walks up fifteen steps to enter and exit his home at least two to three times a day, if not more. He's still living by himself and is very self-sufficient. To see him in this state, for sure, was not normal for us.

I told my dad I couldn't leave him there by himself. I let him know that I was going to take him home with me and make an appointment with the closest urgent care first thing in the morning. This would be a much safer option than exposing him to the general public at that time.

Trying to get my dad from his home to mine was a tedious and strenuous task. He seemed so heavy, and it was a struggle just to lift his legs to move from point A to point B. His ability to even walk five feet without being out of breath was impossible. After about an hour of trying to get him to my car, we finally arrived at my home. My wife came outside to meet me in the car and assist me with getting him into the house and up the stairs so he could prepare for bed.

Once we got him upstairs and settled, my dad looked at me and said something that was very strange to me: "Could you wash me up? " At this request, I knew my dad was really in distress. He had never asked me to assist him with any type of personal hygiene in my entire life. So I washed him up, prayed with him, joked a little to put a smile on his face, thanked him for letting me help him, and then put him to bed. He looked up at me with such a relieved and loving look and said, "Thanks, man." Those two words will always stay with me—just knowing I was there for him in his time of need.

The following morning, I awoke expecting my dad to be past the event from the night before and actually say to me, "Take me home, I'm good now." He always bounces back, so why should this moment be any different? Dad has always been strong. He was my hero and role model for sure. I've always seen him as a monumental figure all my life. However, I was not ready for what I was about to experience. I had no idea that our lives were about to be forever changed and that life as we knew it would be making such a radical shift in only twelve hours.

It was about 6:00 a.m. Monday morning, and I walked into his room to ask him how he was feeling. He said to me, "Can you please help me get adjusted on the bed a little? I'm uncomfortable." When I reached out and grabbed his hand to help shift his body, I felt so much heat coming from him. At that moment, I realized he may have a fever. Rushing to grab the thermometer, my suspicion was correct. Dad had a temperature of 101°F. My wife, who knows how to keep me calm, said, "Babe, don't panic, just give him a Tylenol to help reduce the fever, and let's just monitor him for a little while." And as she always does in her own special way, with her loving voice and beautiful smile, Lawren assured me that Dad would be just fine.

At this point, I decided to call out from work and focus strictly on getting him ready for his doctor's appointment. About two hours later, it was time for me to awaken my dad so I could get him to the local urgent care. I went back into his bedroom to check on him, and when I called his name—"Hey, Pop"—there was only still silence. A second time I called his name, and still no response. Now a nervousness settled on me, and I quickly and gently shook him a little in hopes he was just in a deep sleep due to the Tylenol. He slowly looked up at me as though he was looking directly through me, and all he could do was mumble words that made absolutely no sense. He was not responding well and certainly couldn't answer any simple questions asked of him.

Even as I write this, I am reliving a moment in my life that's still a little emotional for me. At this point, we decided to call 911. Once the medics arrived, they determined that something was going on with his heart, and they would have to transport him to the nearest hospital for further evaluation. Now remember that this was the beginning of the first wave of the COVID-19 pandemic, and hospitals were on lockdown and everyone was in crisis mode. When I told the paramedics that I was going to grab my coat and follow them to the hospital, they quickly informed me that I was not allowed to go due to everything going on with this pandemic. They said someone from the hospital would call me with further instructions and an update.

Now I was in panic mode. They were taking my 84-year-old father to the hospital during a pandemic with so many unknowns and uncertainties. News reports were saying that this virus was not good for seniors, and many were dying because of it. Even though we didn't think Dad had COVID, our concern was that we didn't want him to come in contact with it while being treated at the hospital. With my microbiological background, I immediately knew he would be put into isolation and quarantine without a family member being able to advocate for him. And for sure, we didn't want him to be forgotten about and not receive the proper care and attention he needed. In addition, just knowing that all the hospitals at this time were at full capacity with limited staff due to the situation made it worse. Everything about this was not sitting well with me. How would my dad in his current condition be able to speak on his own behalf?

However, once again the Spirit of the Lord spoke to me and said, "Trust Me." At this point, all I had to hold on to was my faith in God and His ability to get us through this.

It was now Thursday, March 26, 2020, and it had been three days without physically speaking to my dad. We could only wait for occasional updates from his nurses. These calls just couldn't happen fast enough for me. As you can imagine, the wait was very agonizing, and every time the phone would ring, my heart would jump, not knowing what I would hear from the person on the other side of the line. It seemed like all you were hearing was that this pandemic was getting worse and no one could see any light at the end of the tunnel.

Finally, the hospital called with an update on their assessment of my dad. My wife answered the phone, and even though she was not using the speakerphone option, I could hear the conversation. The hospital representative stated that he was suffering from congestive heart failure and that they had removed approximately 160 lbs. of fluid from his body to give him some relief. To make matters worse, they said he also tested positive for COVID-19, and that they were beginning treatments for that.

When that news entered our ears, we both felt as though someone had punched us in the stomach and knocked all of the wind completely out of our lungs. It was like we were in a dream sequence. I just sat on the edge of the bed, stunned by the news that was just delivered. I asked God, how could this be happening to me? And the answer that came back to me was, "I promised you that miracles, signs, and wonders will follow your ministry. How will you ever understand them if you don't experience them?"

I immediately knew that this season of affliction was all a part of my assignment. And where God was taking me would require another level of faith. I just had to go through the process. So many times, we love the promise but hate the process. Always remember, it's the process that develops us so we can effectively manage the promise. The process develops your character to be able to maintain the promise. So many were not able to hold on to the blessings of God because they missed the opportunity for character development.

There were questions and concerns in my mind resonating all over the place. Not only had I just received this news about my dad that shook me to my core, but now I was not feeling at my best. My body muscles were starting to ache, and I was feeling a little sluggish. At that point, my wife told me that I probably needed to get tested to see if I too had contracted COVID-19. You know how we do as men—"No, I'm good," I said, dreading having a swab shoved up my nose, as I had heard the reports that it was a painful thing to go through.

However, I knew she was right, and I needed to protect my family. Swiftly getting out of the bed, I threw some clothes on and nervously made my way to get tested. The whole time I was driving, I was speaking life and coming against any and every sickness that was trying to attack my body. As I was driving, I still couldn't believe all of this was happening. The roads were empty, and you could feel in the atmosphere that something was very different.

I had the car radio on, and all they were talking about were COVID death totals and infection rates from around the globe. I could no longer listen. I turned the radio off and just began to speak God's Word into the atmosphere. I needed to hear His Word in my ears. The Bible says in Romans 10,

> Faith comes by hearing, and hearing by the Word of God.

> — ROMANS 10:17 (KJV)

God's Word is alive. Doubt, unbelief, and fear are birthed when we listen to the opinions of the world and the lies of the devil. It's in our times of trouble that we should remember to always speak God's

Word into the atmosphere. He honors His Word, and His Word always produces what it says it will produce.

Read what God is telling us in Isaiah,

> It is the same with my Word. I send it out, and it always produces fruit. It will accomplish all I want it to, and it will prosper everywhere I send it.

— ISAIAH 55:11 (NLT)

This is a powerful reminder of the undeniable validity of God's Word. Whatever Word God has over my life has success and greatness all over it. Now, I just have to believe it for myself.

Always know that your breakthrough moment is right in your mouth. All you have to do is immediately release it with faith and authority. Whenever we speak or pray the Scriptures, we are changing the atmosphere and reminding God of His promises to us. I was standing on His promises at this point, not the promises of media speculations or the opinions of others. I didn't need to hear anything contrary to good health and long life.

This season would not wound my faith but would reveal the worshipping warrior that was ready for battle. If Satan was sending words of death and destruction, then I knew I had to go to another level in my drive for God. The war was on! Beloved, there is a warrior worshipper inside of you ready to be released. Remember this powerful statement from 2 Corinthians:

> We use God's mighty weapons, not worldly weapons, to knock down the strongholds of human reasoning and to destroy false arguments.

— 2 CORINTHIANS 10:4 (NLT)

Arriving at the urgent care, they would not allow me into the facility; instead, they asked for my cell number and told me to wait in my car until I was called. As I went back to my car with apprehension about being tested, I looked over to my left and saw several white tents in the distance that were set up as triage units. There were individuals in fully covered white protective suits running back and forth as they did their best to take care of the lines of patients there to be tested. Could this really be happening? We were really in the middle of a nightmare. It was something you would only expect to see in a Netflix disaster series. All I kept saying was, "This is crazy."

By this point I was mentally drained. After 30 minutes or so, the doctor called and questioned me over the phone. I explained what I was experiencing, and he stated that because I only had a mild fever of 100°F and no other symptoms, he would prescribe an antibiotic and have me quarantine for 14 days. He also said, "At this point I won't test you because, if you do have COVID-19, you are probably on the back end of it." I was cool with not being tested—no arguments from me on that. With a thank you, I started my car and headed out as fast as possible before he could change his mind. I rushed back home, jumped into bed, quarantined myself from the family, and began to pray for healing in my body. I'm now assessing everything once again. Here I was—fatigued, fevered, frustrated, and not feeling my best. My father was in the hospital by himself with no one to advocate for him. What could possibly happen next?

It's now Saturday, March 28, 2020. The skies are blue, and the sun is shining brightly. It's such a springlike day outside. As I lay in bed, my wife was doing her best to take care of me by wearing a mask and gloves and constantly spraying Lysol. My fever had now increased to 102°F, and my stomach was nauseous. I didn't have an appetite, and everything had a slight bitter taste to it. I wasn't sleeping well, and I was changing my sleepwear because everything was drenched due to the night sweats. There was fatigue in my legs, and my breathing had become a little difficult. There was uncontrolled panting that was happening out of nowhere.

The COVID-19 coverage on social media continued to ramp up, and it's becoming tougher to look at because all that was being posted were stories about people who had lost their lives to this terrible virus —pastors, leaders, first responders, countries, etc. No one was able to escape the grip of this invisible enemy. It had completely consumed everyone's life. All public gatherings were now under mandatory shutdown. Families could only connect with each other through Face-Time or Zoom. Everyone was now forced to adjust to the new normal as it related to how we personally interact. The anxiety level within society had elevated to an alarming rate. Just hearing someone cough or sneeze would put you in fight-or-flight mode.

My phone wouldn't stop ringing. People were calling me literally from all over the world (professionally, personally, and spiritually), talking to me about their mental state, struggles, and the stress that this pandemic had caused in their lives. News about some of our church family who had either contracted the virus or passed away rocked my world. As a pastor, this is an enormous weight—to hear that those you pastor are in need of your support and there's nothing you can do about it. No visits, no hugs, no bedside counseling. And the whole time I was taking all this in, I didn't want to tell anyone— not even my personal family—what was going on in my own life, because I needed to make sure they were encouraged and strengthened by my show of faith and pastoral care.

Not only did I have pastoral responsibilities, but I also held a full-time job as a site operations manager for a major global company. I was running and managing my site team, taking conference calls, making plays, and calling shots from the bed. I can literally remember lying on my back with the computer on my chest, creating Power-Point presentations and participating in global conference calls. Not to mention that I had just received a new assignment several weeks prior to the onset of COVID-19 to oversee our operations in California. I didn't even tell my colleagues or employees what was going on with me because of this new assignment. No one had any idea of all that was happening in my life at this time. It was like a domino effect —just one thing after another.

But in the midst of this storm, I never lost hope or my praise. I had no other choice but to trust that God would get us through this. It was in the midst of this season that God spoke to my heart and let me know that the assignment was greater than the affliction. This personal word to me was paramount. These words would forever change my drive and be the inspiration that would always push me to never stop pursuing greatness. This was a turning point not only in my ministry and career but in my life as a whole. My outlook on everything suddenly shifted upward. A mindset of remaining consistent, committed, and compassionate about this calling on my life was awakened at a different level. Yes, even my corporate career became more of a ministry for me. This season became my season of victory and not defeat. It was an incredible opportunity and not an impossible obstacle. This wasn't designed to destroy me; instead, this experience was going to drive me closer to my divine destiny.

In spite of all I was going through, I had to persevere. What is perseverance? Perseverance is all about having forward motion through endurance. It's refusing to give up or give in to any opposing forces or circumstances—not bowing down to any person, place, or thing that has been put in your path to distract you. This is a mindset that we must possess. We live in a time where so many have made a decision to stop fighting for what they believe in and have worked so hard for, and they've allowed opposition to overtake them and stop their progress.

Many times we forget what Romans says:

 As it is written: 'For your sake we face death all day long; we are considered as sheep to be slaughtered.' No, in all these things we are more than conquerors through Him who loved us.

— Romans 8:36–37 (NIV)

We will have to go through seasons of disappointments and despair, but the Word of God reminds us that we are more than conquerors. To be more than a conqueror literally means that before you even encounter a problem or face a hardship, you have already overcome it through Christ. This is exciting news for you today—just to know that you always live and function from a position of victory. There's no need to worry when you know you've already won. This is the place where you lift your hands and give God praise. You have come out of this as a champion. Yes, I just spoke it into existence. Notice my language of faith to you. Your struggle is a past experience and a distant distraction.

During this time, my worship changed. I found myself singing worship songs in the bathroom while being drenched with tears of adoration to Jehovah God. Sitting on my bed at times with my hands raised toward the heavens or palms opened, I simply thanked God for this experience. Yes, I was thanking Him for this affliction and the glory that would come after this. There was no doubt in my mind that we would survive this. All I knew to do was worship, sing praises, and pray. These moments became teachable moments for me. My faith and reliance on God were growing exponentially. It seemed like the more I worshiped, praised, and cried, the more negative reports would reach my ears about this global event. All of this information began to war against my spirit, but I continued to worship even harder and louder. I was literally digging deep down to find those places where I could encourage myself. My worship became louder than my worries. All of the fear was displaced with unstoppable faith.

I was now preparing and teaching Bible study and Sunday morning sermons online for the church family. I would teach the lesson and then be so drained that I had to sit for fifteen to twenty minutes afterward before I had enough strength just to crawl back upstairs to climb into bed. It was a tough place to be in; however, the assignment was greater than the affliction I was going through. You will hear this term a lot in this book, because God needs us to understand this in order for us as believers to be able to stand in the times we are living in. You have to keep striving and pursuing no matter what comes your way. Giving up and walking away is not an option. Perseverance is a must.

There was a song that kept me through this challenging time:

"Lord, You Are Good" by Todd Galberth. I would just keep reminding God of how good He is even in the midst of the stormy season I was in. It was played in my hearing almost every day and literally became an anthem for me in my times of spiritual battles—even to this day.

Realizing that my incredible wife, Lawren, was also a participant in my assignment, God began to use her to minister to me. She stepped in and supported the vision and purpose of what God called me to do. With daily words of encouragement and powerful prayers, she strengthened me tremendously.

Let me pause for the cause and interject these things to consider: it is so important that you connect with individuals who can be an asset to your assignment and not a liability. Do not just jump into relationships without seeking God for direction and discernment. When you allow people into your intimate space, you are inviting them into your destiny. Kingdom connections are vital to whatever tasks God has assigned to your life. Kingdom connections always outweigh physical connections. Be certain that you are not connecting to people out of your emotional depletion. This is because during your journey with them, things may change. They may walk away, use up the resources they needed from you, or decide that they just don't want to be connected to you anymore. You must be strong enough to continue the defined assignment that God has orchestrated for your life—even when the relationship has dissolved.

I'm reminded of the story of Moses and the importance of having the right kingdom connections when he became weary during a battle.

 Moses' arms soon became so tired he could no longer hold them up. So Aaron and Hur found a stone for him to sit on. Then they stood on each side of Moses, holding up his hands. So his hands held steady until sunset. As a result, Joshua overwhelmed the army of Amalek in battle.

— Exodus 17:12–13 (NIV)

What we can learn from this story is that some of the battles we face can be fierce and ferocious, wearing us out both mentally and physically. But as believers, we should be relentless and determined to overtake the enemy and win the battle at any cost. Here we find Moses incredibly exhausted during this battle with the Amalekites. All of his energy was drained just from interceding for the warriors of Israel during this heated conflict. Moses knew that his assignment was to win this battle. It was part of the process.

Also notice that Aaron, Hur, and Joshua knew the assignment and their participation in it. This kingdom connection was on one accord and working for the same goal. The end result was clear to them: destroy their enemies. They were all aware that their promise was on the other side of the battle. Together they helped Moses persevere in order to accomplish the assignment. The affliction they were up against didn't outweigh the assignment of conquering the promised land.

Aaron and Hur put a stone under him to sit on while one held up his right hand and the other held up his left hand. As long as they held up Moses' hands, Joshua and the warriors of Israel would continue to overtake their enemy, the Amalekites.

Beloved, no matter what challenges may come your way, continue to persevere. Whatever it takes to get the assignment done, make it happen. Don't let anyone shake you or manipulate you out of what God has assigned to your life. Know that God has given you all the necessary tools and connections to accomplish the task at hand. You just have to have faith in God and faith in your abilities.

Knowing who you are in God is such a vital part of your life. Once you come into the full knowledge of who you are and what you've been anointed to do, there is nothing that can stop you from getting it done.

In Philippians 3:14 (NLT), the apostle Paul writes:

 "I press on to reach the end of the race and receive the

heavenly prize for which God, through Christ Jesus, is calling us."

— PHILIPPIANS 3:14 (NLT)

These afflictions are teachable moments for all of us. We learn how to function in trials and times of overwhelming despair. Our anointing is increased, and we are drawn into a deeper relationship with Him. Oftentimes when we are faced with seasons of pain or uncertainties, fear will creep in and try to convince us that everything is working against us. But you must always let your faith override the facts and fears that you may be facing.

Here I was in this new pandemic-driven world trying to figure out how to navigate my way through it—a place where all we had was God and what His Word promised to those who believed. Personally, I had to stay focused and not allow all of what was going on around me to shift the anointed assignment that was at work in me. My assignment as a husband, father, son, pastor, and corporate executive would be done without interference. I chose to believe the report of the Lord and nothing else.

It was at this point that the Holy Spirit brought back to my remembrance Proverbs 18:21 (NLT):

 The tongue can bring death or life; those who love to talk will reap the consequences.

— PROVERBS 18:21 (NLT)

I had to keep reminding myself to speak life into my world and into the world of everyone I communicated with. Perseverance became a part of my everyday walk.

My friend, whenever you are faced with a challenge that seems impossible to conquer, always remember that Satan is the father of lies. Because of this fact, if you hear any negative communication in your spirit that goes against the promises of God, it's a lie from the enemy to discourage and defeat you. Hear what John says:

> He was a murderer from the beginning.
>   He has always hated the truth, because there is no truth in him.
>   When he lies, it is consistent with his character, for he is a liar and the father of lies.

— JOHN 8:44 (NLT)

You can, with confidence, discount anything the devil tries to communicate and plant in your mind because it is not the truth. So in other words, hold on to the report of the Lord—the word of faith. Yes, you are healed, victorious, successful, anointed, powerful, creative, strong, capable, qualified, wealthy, sound, resilient, the head, the lender, and an overcomer—and the list goes on. Believe every word that God has to say about you. Every word that is spoken over your life from the mouth of God. Matthew 24:35 says:

> Heaven and earth will pass away, but my words will never pass away.

— MATTHEW 24:35 (NIV)

God is so faithful. I never deviated from my posture and position of prayer and worship. The language of faith never left me. Negative communications were cut off. The only thing that had my undivided attention was the voice of God. This was a time for me to listen carefully to each movement within the assignment. I strongly believe that because of this obedience to Him, on April 20, 2020, the release came through from my doctor for me to return to the office after five weeks. Five is the number for grace, family! Favor was given to me for sure. Then to top things off, on May 15, 2020, my dad was released to return home after seven weeks—two weeks in the hospital and five weeks in rehabilitation for patients who suffered with COVID. Yes, seven weeks. Seven is God's number of completion.

We made it through this with our hands up. Even when it seems like the battle is a difficult one to endure, just know that you have the ability to complete the assignment. You are a winning survivor. I want to leave you with a Scripture in Psalms:

 Though a mighty army surrounds me, my heart will not be afraid. Even if I am attacked, I will remain confident.

— Psalm 27:3 (NLT)

Tools to Develop a Lifestyle of Perseverance

1. Whenever you are faced with a challenge to your assignment, break that challenge down into small, manageable steps.

Sometimes we can overthink a situation and make the problem bigger than what it is. Learn to manage it in parts. When you take this approach, it won't seem so overwhelming. Whenever a crisis enters our lives, there is a natural tendency to create a false narrative that magnifies the problem in our eyes. Jesus teaches us in Matthew 6:34 (NIV): *"Don't worry about tomorrow, for tomorrow will worry about itself. Each day has enough trouble of its own."*

Let's just concentrate on getting through today. Tomorrow will have its own set of challenges. My friend, prioritize the problems. Remember, there are some challenges to our assignment that can wait to be dealt with. By taking this approach, you will find that you are less stressed about the issue and therefore able to continue moving forward to complete the assignment successfully. Keep in mind that God has given you the grace for the day!

. . .

2. Reconnect with your purpose.

Hebrews 12:1–2 (NIV) declares: *"Let us run with perseverance the race marked out for us, fixing our eyes on Jesus, the pioneer and perfecter of faith."* Sometimes life just happens and we lose sight of the assignment and mandate that God has placed over our lives. It's so important that you are clear about the goal to be achieved and the destiny you are moving toward. If God has placed an assignment on your life, this is an indicator that you are great and well able to accomplish it.

The Scripture says that we are to run with perseverance the race marked out for us. This means that each one of us has a race or assignment given to us. In track and field, individuals often specialize in one type of event. Some are good at hurdles, others at cross-country running, and some at the 100-yard dash. God knows who you are and what He designed you to do. Therefore, there is a race in life specifically designed for you to run and win.

But in order to win the race, you must keep your eyes fixed on Jesus. Runners never look around when running a race, for if they do, they may trip and fall and give up. It's imperative that we keep our eyes on Jesus as we work on our assignments. So no matter what obstacles come to distract us, we don't focus on the distractions, struggles, or frustrations. We stay focused on the goal placed in our hearts.

We can clearly envision what we have been designed to accomplish. I encourage you today: know that this is your race, and it was precisely designed for you to win. Just keep pressing toward the finish line. Don't give up or throw in the towel. The winner's circle is waiting for you. Persevere and complete your purpose.

3. Connection, not isolation.

I'm a firm believer that healthy connections are essential in all of our lives. God desires for all of us to be in relationships that will bring out the best in us. It's critical that we connect with people who will hold us accountable to our life's assignments— individuals who we know will be honest and tell us the truth, even when it's uncomfortable to hear.

I say this because during this process of fulfilling your assignment, you will encounter opposition, obstacles, and in some cases oppression. It is within these moments that you will need someone to remind you of the assignment you are on. This reminder simply redirects us to the end result we are striving to achieve.

The Bible says in Proverbs 27:17 (CEV): *"Just as iron sharpens iron, friends sharpen the minds of each other."* I like to identify these types of connections as kingdom connections. Kingdom connections will always provide emotional, spiritual, and practical support and strength to help us be all that God is requiring of us. We need people who will remind us of our value and unlimited potential.

Now that you've read this chapter, take time to sit with what God has revealed. This is your time to connect what you've read to where you are, and where God is leading you next. Use the following page to reflect, write, and respond.

REFLECTION

1. What am I called to outlast this month?

_____

_____

_____

_____

2. Which voices fuel my faith—and which drain it?

_____

_____

_____

_____

3. How will I break my challenge into small steps?

_____

_____

_____

_____

ACTION

Map your challenge into four bite-size steps. Schedule step #1 in your calendar today.

DECLARATION

Say this declaration with conviction. Let it remind you who you are and what God has called you to do.

Through Christ I am more than a conqueror.
I will outlast every obstacle.

CHAPTER 6

REMAIN

> Therefore, my dear brothers and sisters, stand firm. Let nothing move you. Always give yourselves fully to the work of the Lord, because you know that your labor in the Lord is not in vain.
>
> — 1 CORINTHIANS 15:58 (NIV)

In our ever-turning wheel of life, we always have to be prepared for something to change along the way. It could be a career move, a family crisis, or maybe you just woke up on the wrong side of the bed and you're frustrated with the world. Change is the one thing that I can honestly say is constant. It will happen, and if not handled correctly, we can find ourselves stuck in a moment that can send life spiraling out of control. Often, there is so much noise around us that we easily lose track of where we are as it relates to our assignments and goals. This can lead to uncertainty and cause us to change directions prematurely and possibly abort the seed that God planted in us. Stress and anxiety are often the results when we are not focused and are moving from one extreme to the next.

Have you ever recognized how easy it is for us to say that we are stressed out, frustrated, or overwhelmed? When in actuality, we could be saying, "I got this," "I win," or "I'm not tired." I strongly believe that this mindset is the very device that the enemy will use to discourage and stagnate us. He wants to paralyze us right where we are and prevent us from moving any further toward the winning goal. This is why it's crucial that we learn how to activate the ability to remain.

To remain is a conscious decision to choose stillness when chaos is looking for a reaction. It is to stand in peace when fear demands a fight. To remain means I'm rooted in a deep trust in God, knowing that He holds my world in His hands. It means I'm not shifting my confidence in God even though everything around me is shaken. I'm determined to remain in my God-like character and not compromise my values just because I want my feelings to be validated. How God feels about every given situation is paramount for me. I may move out of the way of the struggle, but I'm not moving out of what I believe is possible to accomplish.

Whenever we remain, we will always increase our endurance, develop spiritual maturity, and put our testimony to the test. It teaches us to hold on until the purpose of the affliction is accomplished. Our faith must be stable and never wavering. It's imperative that we remain on our current course until God instructs us to change. Please understand me, I am not advocating for you to remain in a broken or hurtful situation, but I am saying remain focused on completing the assignment even when you're in the middle of the fight, trying to survive. In today's society, we have been given too many options of compromise and escape, and we don't want to miss the opportunity to grow through it. Yes, I said it, we will grow through remaining on course during times of affliction.

This is one of the reasons why social media is not the best avenue to turn to during struggles. Depending on who has your ear, they will greatly influence your decision-making. It's easy to switch gears and say, "I want to go in a different direction," just because of external influences. How someone else deals with a struggle is not necessarily the exit option for you.

I'm reminded of a story of a little boy who was looking outside his bedroom window one morning and noticed a butterfly trying to emerge from its cocoon. As he gazed at the butterfly, it seemed as though it was having a hard time getting free. The butterfly was vigorously trying to get out. The little boy kept cheering on the butterfly by yelling, "You're almost there, come on, you can do it! " The butterfly seemed to get tired but then started moving and shaking, trying to get free. Pretty soon, the little boy started to feel sorry for the butterfly and decided that it may be in trouble and needed a little help so it could spread its beautiful wings and fly with the grace that all butterflies do. The little boy went outside and gently pulled the walls of the cocoon out far enough so that the butterfly could easily be set free.

All of a sudden, the butterfly fell straight to the ground and was unable to fly. Even though it was flapping its wings, it was just fluttering in the dirt. The little boy thought that he may have damaged its wings, so he and his mother took the butterfly to the biology department of the local college. They explained the situation to the biology professor. The professor smiled and said that the butterfly was released from the cocoon prematurely.

The purpose of the struggle is to strengthen the butterfly's wings by forcing fluids into them, which will help it to fly. The professor told the little boy that by helping the butterfly exit from the cocoon, the butterfly didn't have enough time to complete the developmental process. In other words, the struggle was directly associated with its purpose, and that purpose was to fly.

Metaphorically, this story teaches us that afflictions, difficulties, and challenges are necessary for personal growth, building strength, and helping us achieve our full potential. For us, we must be careful not to allow the opinions of others to talk us out of what God is doing in our lives. We must remain still and see what God is doing in our lives. What lessons are to be learned? What experiences will I gain that I must share with someone else? How is God getting the glory out of this? Remember, there is always purpose in everything we go through. You must remain on task because you will be rewarded for your obedience to the assignment. The struggles may not always be pleasurable, but they are always purposeful.

1 Corinthians 15:58 reminds us to stand firm. Let nothing move you. Always give yourselves fully to the work of the Lord, because you know that your labor in the Lord is not in vain. Because we know that God's Word is true and that we have a destiny, we can stand firm and unshakable in all that we are doing and have been assigned by God to do. We must continue to work hard, knowing that whatever we do right now counts for eternity. This earthly assignment will produce Kingdom results.

Even when you think that all your labor is in vain, because it's not important to everyone else and no one recognizes or acknowledges your efforts, please note that it is always important to God. It doesn't matter if you receive praise or encouragement, because there will be times when you won't be acknowledged for your success. Do not let the accolades of people be the driving force behind your efforts. If the praises of people are what motivate you, you won't remain consistent in your assignment when they stop praising you. People may praise you today and talk negatively about you tomorrow when you are no longer relevant to their needs. Paul says that your labor is not in vain. Just remain on course. Always remember that there is an eternal reward for the work that you do.

When you work under His influence, you can accomplish all things. Let me say to you: remain consistent. Being consistent will always allow you to outlast difficulty. You will never know how committed you are until things get a little rough. Even though you may experience setbacks, you will still reach the expected end if you just remain consistent on the course.

Do you know we serve a consistent God? He is the same yesterday, today, and forevermore. Because God is consistent, our fruit, labor, work, and assignments will also be consistently successful. Here I go again speaking the language of faith, and that's because I believe that God has given each of us everything we will ever need to fulfill His will for our lives on the earth.

Next, we need to remain committed. Commitment is the bridge

we must cross if we want to move from articulating the promises of God to experiencing the promises of God. Do you realize that remaining committed to the assignment is the key that will open the door to your next? Commitment produces growth. Nothing in life truly works without commitment.

When a baby is born, it is the commitment of the parents that determines the growth potential of the baby. The daily routine of feeding, changing, bathing, playing, and teaching helps the baby to grow. But without that kind of commitment, the growth of the baby can become underdeveloped.

Another example of this would be how we budget our finances, take on certain diets to become healthier, pursue higher education to improve ourselves, or invest in our careers and marriages. The list could go on and on. For these things to grow and add value to anything, we must remain committed to them.

The Bible tells us,

> So let's not get tired of doing what is good. At just the right time we will reap a harvest of blessing if we don't give up.
>
> — Galatians 6:9 (NLT)

This verse is such a timely word that encourages us to remain committed to the Kingdom course or journey we are currently traveling. It assures all believers that all the hard work, time, and valuable efforts you are making to complete your assignments will be rewarded in time.

We should not abandon the work that God has assigned us to do, even when we're faced with the most difficult moments. Keeping your eyes on the desired result is what you must always do. If God has assigned you to a task, then know that the task is good. And we never want to give up on good works. You have been placed on the earth to build up, not break down. You have the potential to achieve what others simply dream about.

Jesus says,

 But if you remain in me and my words remain in you, you may ask for anything you want, and it will be granted! When you produce much fruit, you are my true disciples. This brings great glory to my Father.

— JOHN 15:7-8 (NLT)

Again, we see here that there is a great reward for remaining. I love the way Jesus lets us know that if we are connected to Him, we're not just producing fruit, but we will produce much fruit.

Yes, there's a word from God inside of you that will always bring abundance and overflow to whatever assignment you are called to do. Even during times of trouble and crisis, or should I say your dry seasons—you are still able to produce victory and complete the assignment. This is because you are remaining. The season of affliction you may be dealing with is not more powerful than the seed of success that was placed inside of you. This means that there is always an answer to every detour, deterrence, or disturbance that can arise to derail your destiny.

Jesus is committed to you, so remain committed to Him. We are living in a time where people don't remain anymore. They are quick to jump to the next best thing without weighing the cost of leaving so quickly. Longevity seems to be a thing of the past. If actions could talk, they would say:

"If I get bored with a job, I leave, as opposed to trying to create something valuable to enhance my career."

"If I get frustrated in a marriage, I just jump out and try to find someone else, without trying to grow from working through the problem."

People are rarely ever satisfied because, as a society, it's hard for us to remain still and clearly hear the voice of God before we move. We will build trust and credibility when we remain. Whether in personal relationships, work, or pursuing goals, people rely on your behavior and actions when you show that you are remaining stable. If you remain consistent, faithful, and committed, you will be known for that behavior. Others will know what to expect from you, and this in turn will foster strong connections and respect. In professional arenas, this type of attitude will indicate that you are a reliable team leader, which in turn will provide you with long-term success.

Over the years, I've learned to remain. I remember some years ago, I was asked to be a musician for a newly established church in Newark, NJ, called Faith Christian Center. I took on the job and played the organ there for many years. At the time, all I wanted to do was enhance their music ministry, and I loved every moment of it. I was faithful and was on time every Sunday morning without fail. The people treated me well, I got along with the pastor, and life was great.

One day, the pastor decided to leave the church and move on to other opportunities. This caused a split in the church, and the congregation size was reduced within a week. When I showed up the following Sunday, there were only about five people there and no pastor. It was a small storefront church in the heart of the community. It wasn't glamorous or prestigious, but the people who attended were amazing, had a love for the work of the Lord, and a sincere heart for the community.

Just a place where there was an enormous amount of love and determination. I remember the church administrator coming and asking me if I would continue to play and saying that they could no longer afford to pay me for my services. I could sense the hurt and hope in her voice all at once. I replied without hesitation, "No problem, I'm here!" She sighed and said, "Thank you, Darrin." I immediately stated that I would stay and help them rebuild and get back on track. At the time, I had no idea what prompted me to make that statement, but now I know it had to be the Spirit of God at work in me.

I remained, even though I would now be playing for free. That one decision to remain changed the trajectory of my life. To make a long story short, my *yes* to remain ended up being one of the best moves I could have made under those circumstances. I had no idea that God had a much larger plan in mind for me. But I would have to go through this season of affliction in order to have it. By remaining in place, God was literally shaping and molding me to one day become a pastor.

I continued as the Minister of Music at Faith Christian Center for over ten years with no pay. But in return, I gained so much more. I was a part of the search committee for the new pastor, I eventually became the assistant pastor, learned about ministry and serving people from the ground up, was able to get involved with ministry administration and learn how all the business of the church was conducted, and even started an incredible outreach choir there called *Chosen Generation Prison Ministry Choir*, which in turn gave birth to *Chosen Generation Ministries,* of which I am presently the lead pastor.

I mention all of that to say, had I not remained, everything that God wanted to do in my life could have been derailed because I was focused on my wants and desires over His plans for my life. It was a hard journey, but it was worth every struggle. I could have walked away because I was no longer getting paid for my services. I shudder to think that if I had done that over money, I would have lost so much more. And that is the opportunity to be in the perfect will of God and pastor such an incredible congregation, which means so much to me.

In addition, it also gave birth to one of the greatest drummers and producers I know—and that's our son, Aaron "Mr. Lab" Monroe. My *yes* to remain also opened many doors for him to get more involved in the music ministry. Because of this, he has traveled the world performing with some of the best singers and musicians. He even performed on a Grammy-nominated record back in 2010.

So when you have an affliction conflicting with your assignment, you must remember that when you remain faithful to that assignment, you will set into motion blessings and promises that will pass down through generations. It's bigger than you now. God is setting you up for your next!

Now is the time to trust the process, not just the outcome. Remaining helps you surrender the need for immediate results and trust that transformation will happen over time. It's about remaining in place even when you feel disconnected, uncertain, or unworthy— because you will be strengthened through repetition, humility, and resilience.

* * *

Now that you've read this chapter, take time to sit with what God has revealed. This is your time to connect what you've read to where you are, and where God is leading you next. Use the following page to reflect, write, and respond.

REFLECTION

1. Where is God asking me to stand firm and stay faithful?

_____

_____

_____

_____

2. What shortcuts tempt me to leave the process early?

_____

_____

_____

_____

3. Who are my "Aaron and Hur" supports in this season?

_____

_____

_____

_____

ACTION

Choose one arena (marriage, ministry, work). Commit to one consistent behavior for 7 straight days.

DECLARATION

Say this declaration with conviction. Let it remind you who you are and what God has called you to do.

I remain steady, consistent, and committed.
My labor in the Lord is not in vain.

CHAPTER 7

ASSIGNMENT

> Then I heard the Lord asking, 'Whom should I send as a messenger to this people? Who will go for us?' I said, 'Here am I. Send me!'
>
> — ISAIAH 6:8 (NLT)

If I had to open up this conversation concerning assignments from God, I would unequivocally say that our first assignment is to respond in obedience to God. When He gives an individual a specific assignment, it is a unique purpose and work that God has entrusted to their life. It is truly humbling when God selects you to do a job within His Kingdom.

I strongly believe that it's one thing for us to trust God, but it's at a totally different level when God can trust us to fulfill purpose and assignment. This within itself should never be taken lightly. It's not about doing what we want, but about synchronizing our actions with His will.

> For we are God's masterpiece. He has created us anew
> in Christ Jesus, so we can do the good things He
> planned for us long ago.
>
> — Ephesians 2:10 (NLT)

This verse lets us know that our assignments are not random or haphazard events, but were designed with great intention before you and I were even conceived. Walking in this level of design takes obedience and faith.

Back in 1990, the Lord birthed in my heart the vision to start an outreach community choir that would focus on outreach-based functions. It started with about seven singers and just me on piano. After a year, the group grew to about 40 voices with a full-piece band. No words can describe what we were feeling. It was an exciting time, and we were all in our twenties—a group of energetic young people who were just excited to see people say *yes* to Jesus.

We traveled within the state of New Jersey, going to whatever prison, correctional facility, hospital, or street corner that would allow us to set up, sing, and minister. It was so satisfying to know that we were inspiring those we encountered in such a powerful and positive way. I knew this was an assignment from God. Helping people and music were two passions that drove me at that time.

On the other side of this, I was a full-time lab technician at an orange juice manufacturing company. I enjoyed what I did and felt as though I was good at it. Science and analytical thinking are another passion of mine. My career was taking off, and the company created a position for me entitled Assistant Technical Director. I was excited that all of these wonderful things were happening all at once.

The company flew me down to Winter Haven, Florida, to interview for the position. When I arrived, they told me I would be getting a large raise with great bonus potential. I was assigned a realtor who took me house hunting. I was shown all these new homes with screened-in swimming pools attached, beautiful neighborhoods for raising children, and more. Life couldn't be better. This assignment from the company was everything I felt the American dream was about.

But then reality began to hit. I had two assignments of which I could say God opened the door and made a way. But in this case, I had to make a choice. One assignment would relocate me to Florida, while the other would keep me in New Jersey, living in my current apartment in the house my parents owned. This was a tough decision, because both opportunities could work, and I could justify that both were a blessing. However, something in my world would have to shift.

I prayed and consulted God as well as others that I trusted. The natural side said this was a guaranteed wealth changer and career bump, but the spiritual side thought about the people and ministry I would leave behind.

It was a difficult decision to make, especially when there were so many opinions in my ear saying, "Take the money and lifestyle change." Personally, in my heart, I was humbled by the fact that this billion-dollar company created a position and opportunity for this kid from Jersey City, New Jersey. But deep inside, my heart wasn't settled on leaving.

I remember the night before I had to make my final decision. I couldn't sleep. If I told them *yes*, then the ball would start rolling, and I would have to inform the choir that I was relocating. If I told them no, then there was a good chance I might lose my job, and I certainly would have wasted the company's time and money going through the interview process. What would they think of me, then?

Well, I turned down the newly created position for what I believed was God's true assignment for my life, and that was to impact and influence lives in New Jersey. Yes, after six months the company let me go. It was a hard pill to swallow. But God has a way of turning things around in our favor.

When I was let go, I didn't go kicking and screaming or cursing everyone out in rage and anger. I thanked them for all of the opportunities and stated, "If you ever need any support from me, I will make myself available."

Sounds too nice, doesn't it? Well, consider this truth:

Whenever you are moving in your assignment and purpose,
nothing and no one will be able to pull you out of your
character, because you are confident in your purpose.

Even when I moved on, I kept in contact with those who I felt
were responsible for me losing my job. I would still send them gift
boxes every Christmas from the company I was working for.

About ten years later, I received a call from that same company
that had laid me off. They asked me to come back to start up their
Quality Assurance Department. I accepted the position, but this time
it was on my terms. They gave me back the years that I had originally
worked for them, started me off with four weeks of annual vacation,
and added a bonus package that was perfect. After being there for
seven years as Quality Manager, they asked me if I would take over
the entire facility as the plant manager. Of course, I took it, and the
rest is history.

To put the icing on the cake, I now sit in the office of the man who
let me go some fifteen years ago. And to add to that, that outreach
choir evolved into a church of which I'm now the lead pastor. Some of
those same individuals who started with me as singers are still
working with me to win souls and change lives. We are a family. I
shudder to think about how one decision could affect so many lives.
Had I jumped on that Florida assignment, I would have missed what
God really wanted to do through me.

Going through that season was an affliction for me because it was
incredibly stressful and frustrating. Many sleepless nights were spent
trying to decide. So many lives were hanging in the balance. Today, I
can truly say, "To God be the glory for being obedient to His voice and
assignment." You can't always measure success by material things.
Jesus said,

 Seek the Kingdom of God above all else, and live right-
eously, and He will give you everything you need.

— MATTHEW 6:33 (NLT)

God's plans and assignments over your life will always take you higher if you don't allow your emotional desires to override your spiritual desires. I understood that keeping focused on His plan would benefit me and those around me in the long run. The way I see it, everything attached to me wins! I just have to make sure I'm in position to make it happen. Every experience is designed to expose the best in us, especially those that we gain from our assignments.

Any assignment from God will present itself at the intersection of your passions, skills, and opportunities. Also, be prepared to be stretched beyond your comfort zone. We need to be stretched, because when this happens, it reminds us that we must depend on God's strength to present a finished work. God will not ask us to do anything we are not able to do. He will always equip us with the necessary tools and resources to fulfill the task.

As amazing as you are, there will still be moments when you don't even recognize your extraordinary ability to carry out the function. But through obedience, what was lying quietly within you will awaken and develop into a mature masterpiece that will bring glory to God.

Having assignments from God can at times feel intimidating, because the assignment will always appear bigger than your capacity to complete it. You must see the impossibility and declare that it is possible.

When trying to recognize the tasks that God put into my heart to do, I would always take a personal inventory and eliminate anything that would interfere with that assignment. Life today is so inundated with so many different things. Even when we take a vacation nowadays, it's really not a vacation, because we are locked into a fast-paced lifestyle—checking emails, texts, calendar updates, Zoom meetings, video conference calls, global activity, and need I say more? In addition, you have family, friends, and in some cases, ministry demands. You have to learn how to prioritize and maintain balance.

The Word of God says,

> We must throw off every weight that slows us down, especially those sins that just won't let go.

— HEBREWS 12:1 (CEV)

If you notice, it says "we." That means there are some things that you must eliminate—an action initiated by you. In other words, make an intentional effort to eliminate the non-essentials in your life. The non-essentials are the things that keep us busy but don't add any value to our lives.

If what I'm doing is not making me a better person or helping to build a solid foundation on which to grow, then maybe I need to move that element out of my life. Sometimes we will do things simply out of tradition or comfort. They become distractions and obstacles that pull our attention away from what we're supposed to accomplish. Once you remove them, you will find yourself being fulfilled in so many areas. Please note: if you don't miss what you removed, then don't restart it. And yes, this includes people, places, or things. Sometimes we don't need deliverance; we just need discipline.

Make it a daily routine to excel at what really matters most. Have good time management. Also, live on purpose. Always be intentional when it comes to attacking God-given assignments, and always choose good priorities. Lay everything out in a systematic manner that is achievable. Never be afraid to embrace the new things that God wants to introduce us to. The reason many of us don't embrace new ideas is because it requires change, and change requires work. But remember: change is like the raw material of opportunity. And without raw materials, you can't develop a finished product.

When trying to understand what our assignments are, I would say you must first recognize the assignment. It will be something that you have a passion for. The assignment isn't given to you because the work is finished; it's given because you are well able to take it to the next level. There is something that God has planted within you that no one else has. You are uniquely designed by God with the task in mind. And until you step in and touch it, it will remain unfinished.

When you recognize exactly what it is you were called to do, what was difficult for everyone else will come naturally for you. I'm not saying it will be an easy road. Anything worth having is worth the fight.

But what I will say is that God will give you wisdom, insight, ingenuity, creativity, and everything else needed to get it accomplished. And when you recognize that without Him it can't be done, and you give Him the glory for its success, then what you touch will grow exponentially. There will be such an overflow that everyone around you and connected to you will benefit from the impact of your obedience.

The next thing that we need to do is respond with obedience. This is an area where many of us will fail or procrastinate. God has given us clear instruction on what to do, but we are more focused on the affliction than the assignment, and then we become stuck. Whenever we allow our emotions to get caught in the moment, it numbs our spiritual awareness. The physical pain we are dealing with often overrides our spiritual drive. Assignments always require action, not just understanding.

James tells us,

 But don't just listen to God's word. You must do what it says. Otherwise, you are only fooling yourselves.

— James 1:22 (NLT)

When we move on God's Word and carry out the assignment, the end result will always be: we win. Always be ready to say *yes,* even when we don't have all the answers.

And finally, rely on His strength. His strength is made perfect in our weakness. This means that His power is most evident when we acknowledge our limitations and totally rely on Him. Many times, we think everything gets accomplished because of our skills, gifts, and talents. Yes, they play a part, but it's His anointing on those things that makes the difference and gives us the complete win. He wants to know that we truly depend on His direction and guidance.

This is a call to humility and dependence, not a call to our own ability alone. We work with God to get the assignments completed. It's imperative that we are aware that He is with us. If we have this mindset, then we won't get discouraged or defeated. Even when the thorns of life come to aggravate me, I'm still able to function because I'm relying on Him whenever I feel myself getting weak or at that point where I want to throw in the towel.

It's important to remember that you are too important to the world to allow circumstances and situations to cause you to abort the assignment. Finally, remember that our assignments from God will always have global implications. Every life you impact has a multiplicity of other lives connected to it. By touching one person, you can possibly touch a million people. This is why it's important to follow God-given assignments.

I want to encourage you that you are greater than your struggles—so don't throw in the towel and quit. You have to keep the bigger picture in view. When you commit to your divine assignment, you won't only find personal fulfillment, but you will also become a tremendous blessing to everyone around you. You walk with great purpose inside of you that impacts and influences the lives of so many. Do you realize that you are the answer to someone's prayer?

Stand firm and don't let your faith waver. Have confidence in your abilities as well as the gifts God has imparted into each of us. In all that you do, give God the glory and stay in the fight. You will live through this, survive, and thrive, because…

Your assignment is greater than your affliction!

* * *

Now that you've read this chapter, take time to sit with what God has revealed. This is your time to connect what you've read to where you are, and where God is leading you next. Use the following page to reflect, write, and respond.

Reflection

1. Where do my passions, skills, and opportunities intersect?

_____

_____

_____

_____

2. What non-essentials must I throw off to run my race?

_____

_____

_____

_____

3. How will I rely on His strength, and not just my talent?

_____

_____

_____

_____

Action

Identify one God-assignment. Remove one weight this week (time, habit, or commitment) to make room for it.

Declaration

Say this declaration with conviction. Let it remind you who you are and what God has called you to do.

> _Here am I. Send me._
> _I obey quickly, steward faithfully,_
> _and rely on God's strength._

CHAPTER 8

TRUST

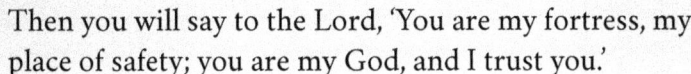

Then you will say to the Lord, 'You are my fortress, my place of safety; you are my God, and I trust you.'

— PSALM 91:2

Tuesday, November 4, 2025, started off as expected. I had a full night of rest, woke up feeling refreshed, and then rolled out of bed at 6 a.m. I fell to my knees to pray and thank God for blessing me to see another day. Lawren and I had our routine morning greeting and kiss as I threw on my clothes and prepared myself to head down to the office. This day was special because I was having some new lab equipment delivered, which for me means new toys to play with and a new skill to learn. Quickly making my way downstairs like a child on Christmas morning, I was headed to the door. As I opened up my garage, it was a beautiful fall day. The sky was vibrantly blue, and there were no signs of clouds anywhere. If I had the words to describe the view, you could say it was postcard-perfect. The morning air was cool and crisp, and the fallen leaves crackled under every step you took. The birds were singing, and it seemed as though nothing could possibly go wrong.

As I got on the highway entrance, the Lord laid on my heart to contact my aunt, who was very ill, to check in and have a word of prayer with her. My cousin had spent the night with her, so I knew it would be easy to communicate with her. My aunt was not verbal at the time; however, I felt in my heart she could hear me. When I asked my cousin how her rest was last night, she stated that Auntie had a good night, but she didn't open her eyes or respond much. She was still very weak. I asked my cousin to please put the phone up to her ear so she would be able to hear me praying for her. As I was praying, I could hear her breathing loudly and rapidly. It sounded like she was trying to release a word from her mouth but just didn't have the strength to do so. All she could do was grunt and moan during her struggle to breathe. After I completed the prayer, we just began to worship in her ear and thank God for all that He does for us. This was a special moment for us. While in the midst of worship, Auntie made a loud sound and exhaled. The room grew quiet, and I asked my cousin, "Did she just stop breathing?" She said, "Darrin, I think she just left us." I immediately pulled to the side of the road to assess the situation, and my concerns were confirmed. She had transitioned just that fast and was no longer with us.

This was such a surreal moment. I was trying to process what had just happened, what the next steps were, and how to manage my work assignment for the day. It seemed overwhelming at the moment, but it was then I had to slow down and begin to trust God and trust the process that He was going to guide me through. He's never failed me before, so why should I think He would fail me now? I had to relinquish any idea that I was not able to handle this surprising affliction that came in like a violent storm. It was a life-changing moment. Life as I knew it for so many years had changed instantly and would never be what it was. I was shaken to the core but still had to move forward. So I pulled over to the side of the road, gathered my thoughts, and asked God for direction. My next steps would allow me to handle this affliction in champion style.

First, I let my wife know so she could assist me in managing this crisis and be my backup. She always comes through strong. That's the value of teamwork. Next, I contacted the nurse and instructed them to confirm my thoughts that my aunt had transitioned. This was all I could do since I wasn't there physically. I hurriedly continued to the office to begin preparing for my weekly management meeting. Once I completed my PowerPoint slides and metrics, I contacted my manager to inform him of the situation and gave him a heads-up that I might have to leave the meeting to attend to this current family emergency. He gave me a pass and told me to go home. However, I decided to stay and work through the process because I knew God would give me the wisdom and strength. This is how much I trusted Him in this. There was no way I could manage this situation without God's guidance. As I walked through each step, the more and more I felt at peace, and I truly believed it was because I spoke to myself, saying, "I can do this." You have to not only trust God but also your ability to overcome the challenge.

The importance of understanding assignment really hit me when I attended the management meeting, which my team was not expecting me to. I presented and conducted myself as I always do. I may not have been as vocal due to all the things that were weighing heavy on me, but I didn't allow the affliction to consume me. Later that day, I received text messages from my colleagues asking if I was okay. They were literally wondering if the report of a family death was communicated incorrectly because I didn't allow the circumstance to change my character or affect my ability to function in purpose. My affliction actually opened a door to witness about God's goodness in spite of tough moments. The strength exhibited was a light and inspiration for all those around. It also showed my colleagues that we are designed to bend at times but not break. This will always happen when you put trust in God and His process.

Every believer will eventually walk through a season when life no longer makes sense. The plans we cherished unravel, the prayers we've spoken seem to go unanswered, and the road ahead becomes uncertain. In those moments, it's sometimes difficult to activate your faith. On the other side of the coin, it's always easy to trust God when everything is coming together as we've hoped. But real trust—the kind that matures and deepens—will always take root in adversity or affliction. When the seed of trust is planted, it grows strongest in the soil of confusion, heartbreak, and waiting. Trusting God when life hurts is not a denial of reality. It is the courageous act of saying, "Even here, even now, I will believe You are good and You are God." Trust does not always come naturally; it develops and matures over time. It's whenever we give up control and allow God to lead us one step at a time—through valleys as much as through mountaintops—and it's in those valleys that He teaches us not only who He is but who we are in Him.

Afflictions rarely give advance notice. A phone call changes everything. A letter arrives with disappointing news. A doctor clears their throat before speaking words that will change the direction of our lives. We find ourselves suddenly swept into seasons we never would have chosen. In those moments, the natural question arises: Where is God? King David knew that feeling well. In Psalm 13:1, he cried out, "How long, Lord? Will You forget me forever?" Those are not the words of a faithless individual; they are the words of an honest one. Faith does not silence our pain; it just brings it before God. David teaches us that trust and affliction can coexist. To trust God doesn't mean to never feel the pressure of the storm; it means to keep turning toward Him even when we do.

Another narrative comes to mind when the disciples were caught in the storm on the Sea of Galilee. Jesus was asleep in the boat. The waves rose, the winds roared, and fear took over. "Teacher," they shouted, "don't You care if we drown?" (Mark 4:38, NIV). That question echoes in every storm of life that we encounter. But what did Jesus do? He stood, spoke peace to the storm, and then asked, "Why are you so afraid? Do you still have no faith?" (v. 40, NIV). Notice that Jesus didn't rebuke them for waking Him—He rebuked the storm, then reminded them of who He was. In times of trouble, God's goal is not always to remove the storm immediately but to reveal His presence while we are engulfed in it. Trust begins when we realize that even when God seems silent, He is not absent.

Every affliction will test the strength of our trust. Peter wrote,

"These trials will show that your faith is genuine. It is being tested as fire tests and purifies gold" (1 Peter 1:7, NLT). As I stated in an earlier chapter, fire does not destroy gold—it refines it. In the same way, afflictions do not destroy real faith; they strengthen it. When everything is going well, we can mistake comfort for faith. The benefit of adversity is that it forces us to let go of illusions of control. It humbles us. It teaches us that God is not merely the God of our blessings, but He is also the God of our brokenness.

May I suggest that the hardest part of going through a rough season is surrendering what we cannot control? We always want to know the why, the when, and the how. Yet God often calls us to exhibit trust even when we don't have full understanding. That's where faith becomes real. Trust doesn't come from knowing how everything will work out; it comes from knowing the One who is able to work it out. Another way of describing trust is simply found in the word *surrender*. Surrender is not giving up—it's really giving over. It's totally letting go of the reins of our control and placing the reins into the hands of our Heavenly Father. This is not always an easy action— it is daily, deliberate, and can many times be painful. But it can lead to a peace that cannot be found any other way.

Isaiah 26:3 promises, "You will keep in perfect peace those whose minds are steadfast, because they trust in You." Notice that peace follows trust. When we stop trying to control the outcome and instead rest in God's sovereignty, we begin to experience the calm of His presence even in the midst of the storm.

When Trust Feels Impossible

I'm sure there is someone who is reading this chapter and saying that it's impossible to trust in the way you are describing. To that, I say yes, there are moments when trusting God feels beyond us—when grief, disappointment, or fear seem too heavy to carry. But may I suggest that in those times, it helps to remember that trust is not about feeling strong; it's about choosing faith even in weakness. Even our Lord and Savior Jesus shows us how to advance through affliction. In the

Garden of Gethsemane, Jesus Himself faced anguish so deep that His sweat fell like drops of blood. He prayed, "Father, if You are willing, take this cup from Me; yet not My will, but Yours be done" (Luke 22:42). Even the Son of God wrestled with surrender. And in that moment, He showed us what perfect trust looks like—not the absence of struggle, but the willingness to yield.

My friend, when you cannot find words to pray, whisper what Jesus did: "Not my will, but Yours." That simple surrender keeps the door of trust open, even when every emotion pulls the other way. Even when I prayed for my aunt, I knew what I wanted, and that was for her to get up off her place of sickness and recover. However, my prayer included those words: "Not my will, but let Your will be done." And I had to trust His will over mine. This is how I was able to function in my assignments that day in spite of the affliction. I refused to let pain have the final word on that day. God's goodness will always be deeper than our sorrows and His purposes bigger than our understanding.

Another perspective on this is knowing that when you put complete trust in God, there will always be a blessing on the other side of affliction. They don't last forever. Even though the night may feel endless, the morning eventually comes, and then we get a brand-new opportunity to work through the process and learn from our mistakes. When we begin to look back over our lives and take a self-evaluation, we will see the fingerprints of God all over our journey. The things that we thought would destroy us are the very things that shaped us. We were transformed by affliction and adversity.

Trust transforms how we see ourselves and others. We become gentler with people's pain because we've known our own. We stop rushing God's process in others because we remember how patiently He worked with us. Our faith becomes less about performance and more about relationship. Every trial becomes a testimony. Every valley becomes a story of God's faithfulness. And when others walk through their own dark seasons, our lives can point them to the One who never left us in ours.

We serve a God who holds us steady. If you find yourself in a season of affliction right now—if the way forward feels uncertain or the weight feels unbearable—please know this: God has not abandoned you. His silence does not mean absence. His delays do not mean indifference. He is closer than you think, working in ways you cannot yet see. Trusting God doesn't require that you understand everything. It just requires that you rest in the truth that He does.

The same God who was faithful to Joseph in the prison, to David at Ziklag, to Esther in the palace, and to Jesus on the cross—is faithful to you now. You may not see the full picture yet, but one day you will look back and see how His hand guided you, protected you, and shaped you through every trial. Hold on. Keep trusting. Keep walking. Continue pressing forward. You are not forgotten, and this season will not define you. God's purpose for you is still alive, and His promises still stand. You can trust God!

* * *

Now that you've read this chapter, take time to sit with what God has revealed. This is your time to connect what you've read to where you are, and where God is leading you next. Use the following page to reflect, write, and respond.

REFLECTION

1. Think about a season in your life when trusting God felt difficult. What emotions surfaced, and how did that experience shape your faith?

_____

_____

_____

_____

_____

_____

_____

_____

_____

_____

_____

_____

_____

2. In what ways have you seen God's hand working behind the scenes, even when the situation didn't make sense at the time?

_____

_____

_____

_____

_____

_____

_____

_____

_____

_____

_____

_____

_____

3. What areas of your life do you still find hard to surrender completely to God's control?

_____
_____
_____
_____
_____
_____
_____
_____
_____
_____
_____
_____
_____
_____
_____

ACTION

Instead of trying to fix it yourself, take a few minutes each day to pray, "Lord, I trust You with this." Write down any peace, clarity, or lessons you experience as you intentionally release control to Him.

DECLARATION

Say this declaration with conviction. Let it remind you who you are and what God has called you to do.

I may not see it all, but I trust the One who does.
God is guiding, sustaining, and strengthening me.

Your Journey Continues

It is my desire that this book will inspire you to continue moving forward, especially when you're faced with opposition and obstacles. I want you to realize that you have been designed by God to be able to conquer anything that should come into your life to defeat you. Afflictions will always be an undeniable part of life's journey. There's no way to totally escape this fact. However, it's important to stay alert and focused, as they can show up in our lives in many different forms. They can appear as pain, rejection, disappointment, delays, despair, etc.

Yet, as overwhelming as they may make us feel, we have comfort in knowing that they are temporary events. I'm thankful that no season of suffering we may face will last forever, and there is no trial that we will encounter that has the power to cancel the assignments God has placed in our hands to do. We may not always be able to avoid afflictions; however, when they do appear, please understand that they were never designed to be the measure of who we are or where we are in this world.

I believe that every affliction is instrumental in maturing us. They will never be able to define us. What truly defines us is our willingness to rise high above the affliction while yet remaining faithful to the assignment in order to bring it to an expected end. No season of affliction will last forever, and the plans of God for us will prevail.

2 Corinthians reminds us,

 For our light affliction, which is but for a moment, worketh for us a far more exceeding and eternal weight of glory.

— 2 CORINTHIANS 4:17 (KJV)

When the Apostle Paul penned this letter to the Corinthian church, his perspective totally flipped human reasoning. He wasn't dismissing pain or pretending that suffering or afflictions are not real. Instead, he encouraged them that the struggles experienced will not last forever. They do have an expiration date.

Paul wants us to keep our eyes fixed on the bigger purpose. Going through struggles is all a part of God's redemptive process. Temporary pain clearly becomes a bridge that carries us to eternal reward. We are to be transformed through what we are dealing with. Don't waste a good affliction! They work for us, not against us, whenever we have enduring faith. They will always build perseverance, shape our character, and deepen our reliance on God. And that is all about being faithful to the assignment. It's our obedience in the midst of the struggle that carries the greater weight. It speaks volumes about who you really are and what you're capable of achieving. Every time we push forward in our faith, we are declaring to the world that God's purpose for our lives is greater than the weight of the trials we're going through.

Could it be that the very afflictions we are facing are not meant to destroy us, but to prepare us? For example, whenever you have gold, fire does not destroy it; fire refines it. The heat separates all of the impurities from the gold. And the refiner patiently watches the metal until he is able to see his own reflection in the molten liquid, indicating that it is pure.

Now, let's apply that process to the subject matter. No matter what comes our way, we can rest in knowing that God is always there with us. And just like the refiner, He may allow the heat of our afflictions to bring out the best in us so that He can truly see His reflection in us. You see, these struggles that we experience should always conform us into the image of His Son, Jesus.

You will never know how to deal with struggles until you experience struggles. James states,

 Consider it pure joy, my brothers and sisters, whenever you face trials of many kinds, because you know that the testing of your faith produces perseverance. Let perseverance finish its work so that you may be mature and complete, not lacking anything.

— JAMES 1:2-4 (NIV)

The writer wants us to be very intentional and choose joy in the midst of trials because of what God is seeking to accomplish through them. What you're dealing with is not new. People have survived it before, and so will you. Joy is not about feelings; it's all about perspective. When we focus on trying to be happy as opposed to having joy, we will always be disappointed.

Having joy means that no matter what is occurring externally, internally I'm still good and able to function without allowing my emotions to take control. I also like the way he outlines, "whenever you face trials," which lets us know they will happen at some point, so you can't be surprised when they do. You just have to know that they are making you even stronger—physically, emotionally, and spiritually.

Let's go even deeper. It's not enough just to survive this, but you must let it complete what it was designed to do for you. Believe it or not, it's working for your good! Sometimes we can abort a blessing because we were afraid to endure the season of affliction.

What you are dealing with right now may seem like it's too much to handle. The weight of it all is bearing down on you, and you feel like calling it quits. Know that this is not the end of your story. Please don't insert a period where there should be a comma. God is not done with you yet, and you still have chapters to complete in this book we call life.

What God has placed inside of you carries eternal weight, and completing the assignment is far more important than the struggle you are faced with. Continue to press forward, keep the faith, and make a conscious effort to choose obedience over comfort. Always remember that your purpose is greater than your pain.

Your assignment is greater than your affliction!

Acknowledgments

This journey would not have been possible without the incredible people God has placed in my life to encourage, strengthen, and support me along the way. I am forever grateful for each of you who believed in me, prayed for me, and stood by me through every season.

To my wife, *Lawren*, my heart's quiet strength: You are the wind in my sails and my anchor when needed. You are a gift beyond expression.

To my parents, *Sadie and Bob Monroe*: You taught me the value of hard work, the warmth of kindness, and what it means to be a man of integrity. I'm so blessed to have you as my mom and dad. Miss you dearly!

To *Aaron*, my son: You're the kind of son every father dreams of. You're always there when I need you, and your determination inspires me to keep pursuing my dreams. My musical genius!

To my daughters *Rose, Stephanie, and Trinity:* You are the very definition of hard work and determination. Thank you for being shining examples of what's possible. You inspire "Pop" every single day!

To my spiritual parents, *Bishop George and Pastor Mary Searight*:

Thank you for teaching me the true meaning of ministry, marriage, and balance. You're simply the best!

To my mother-in-love, *Dr. Mamie Bridgeforth:* Thank you for loving me as your own and embracing me as a son. You enrich my life every day!

To my aunt (mom), *Colonel Nancy A. Henderson*: Thank you for being the embodiment of unconditional love and service to our entire family. You are an amazing woman!

To my *Chosen Generation Church Family*: Thank you for your prayers, support, and dedication. I love being connected to you. *Love you all to life*!

About the Author

Darrin Monroe is the Lead Pastor of Chosen Generation Ministries, where he has dedicated decades to serving others through faith-based leadership and transformative outreach programs. His ministry extends to diverse communities, including active engagement in prison ministry and other initiatives designed to  bring hope, healing, and restoration to those in need. He is passionate about empowering others to walk boldly in their God-given purpose.

Beyond his pastoral calling, Pastor Monroe is a seasoned corporate executive with a strong background in the biological sciences. His professional career is marked by a proven ability to build, mentor, and develop leaders across multiple disciplines. His leadership workshops has helped major corporations achieve higher levels of productivity.

Drawing upon both his spiritual insight and executive experience, Pastor Monroe inspires individuals to embrace their divine assignments with perseverance, discipline, and faith, which in turn empowers them to accomplish God's purpose even in the face of adversity and affliction.

Pastor Monroe, along with his wife, Dr. Lawren Monroe, are the proud parents of Aaron, Rose, Stephanie, and Trinity.